Mastering Conversation Skills

Goodbye Awkwardness. Learn to Master the Art of Conversation and Become A Great Communicator, Even if You've Always Been Shy or Hate Small Talk

© Copyright 2019 by _____ - All rights reserved.

The following book is reproduced below with the goal of providing information that is as accurate and reliable as possible. Regardless, purchasing this book can be seen as consent to the fact that both the publisher and the author of this book are in no way experts on the topics discussed within and that any recommendations or suggestions that are made herein are for entertainment purposes only. Professionals should be consulted as needed prior to undertaking any of the action endorsed herein.

This declaration is deemed fair and valid by both the American Bar Association and the Committee of Publishers Association and is legally binding throughout the United States.

Furthermore, the transmission, duplication, or reproduction of any of the following work including specific information will be considered an illegal act irrespective of if it is done electronically or in print. This extends to creating a secondary or tertiary copy of the work or a recorded copy and is only allowed with the express written consent from the Publisher. All additional rights reserved.

The information in the following pages is broadly considered a truthful and accurate account of facts and as such, any inattention, use, or misuse of the information in question by the reader will render any resulting actions solely under their purview. There are no scenarios in which the publisher or the original author of this work can be in any fashion deemed liable for any hardship or damages that may befall them after undertaking information described herein.

Additionally, the information in the following pages is intended only for informational purposes and should thus be thought of as universal. As befitting its nature, it is presented without assurance regarding its prolonged validity or interim quality. Trademarks that are mentioned are done without written consent and can in no way be considered an endorsement from the trademark holder.

Table of Contents

Introduction 7

Chapter 1 - Establishing Likability 10

The Confirmation Bias 10

The Qualities & Behaviors that Make You Instantly Likable 12

What Determines Likable Behavior? 15

The Seven Bad Habits that are Making You Unlikable 16

Chapter 2 - The Basics of Good Conversation 21

How to Make Great First Impressions 21

Win at Small Talk with the ARE Model 24

Three Essential Ways to Get Along with Anyone You Meet 25

Six Tips for Resisting Shyness and a Lack of Confidence 28

Chapter 3 - Igniting Exceptional Interactions 32

Conversation Topics & Tips for Every Possible Scenario 32

The Worst Mistakes You Can Make in a Conversation 36

Ideas to Steer Clear of Boring Conversations 41

Three General Rules for Sparking an Interesting Conversation 43

Chapter 4 - Cultivating Charisma and Magnetism 45

The Thirteen Secrets to Developing a Magnetic Personality 45

All You Need to Know About the Trifecta of Charm 51

Three Steps to Becoming a More Interesting Person 57

Chapter 5 - Knowing Your Audience 59

Microexpressions 59

The Six Types of Communicators & How to Win Them Over 62

Conversation Tips for Special Audiences 66

Chapter 6 - Building Deep Connections **68**

Conversation Tricks to Instantly Build Rapport with Someone *68*

How to Form Meaningful Relationships *70*

The Habits of Emotionally Intelligent People *72*

Why Self-Compassion is Important for Healthy Relationships *75*

Chapter 7 - Difficult Situations & Social Blunders **77**

How to talk your way out of difficult or awkward situations *77*

Coping with Difficult Personalities *81*

When is it okay to lie? *86*

Chapter 8 - Using Conversation to Get What You Want **88**

Subtle ways of showing dominance *88*

Persuasion Techniques for all Situations *90*

Three Tricks to Seduce Someone through Conversation *93*

Six Highly Effective Tips for Successful Negotiations *96*

Conclusion **99**

Introduction

I know the real reason you opened this book: you're desperate to see change in your day-to-day life. You're bored of lackluster social interactions, a dead-end career and you're disappointed by your strained or unfulfilling relationships. You know it can get better - you've seen other people develop the kind of relationships you desire - and you want to own that kind of social influence now.

This may surprise you, but you're not the only one who feels this way. Leagues of people across the world dream of these same changes and, like you, they have a hunch that the solution lies in amping-up their social abilities. Like you, they want to be a conversational master.

But the good news is, you're already one step ahead of them.

Why? It's simple. You've taken the first step. You've opened this book. You're about to commit to greater achievements and more powerful relationships – and that makes you a tad smarter than the rest. Congratulations on getting a little closer to your goals.

Perhaps you're awkward and shy. Perhaps, you constantly feel overpowered in social settings, like your presence doesn't matter. You never know the right thing to say and it feels like you're always one beat behind the rest.

Or perhaps, you're not socially awkward at all, you simply want to wield more influence over your peers and make a stronger impact on everyone you meet. You've seen the way some people get what they want using only their words, and you want to experience what it's like. I'll tell you now, this experience can be yours with some practice and expert wisdom. It's not as difficult as it looks, you just need the right training.

Whatever stage you're at, whether you're a timid wallflower or a fairly confident conversationalist, this book will take you to the same destination: the top of your communication game. This book will show you the entire spectrum, from the very basics of good conversation to the advanced tools of persuasion and influence. We'll break down language, behavior, and personality into their digestible parts - and you'll achieve mastery over them all. You'll learn how to befriend, seduce, and resolve conflict with only the magic of communication. And by the end of your training, you'll know how to navigate nearly every situation known to man. From the difficult, strained scenarios to the intimate and deep connections.

Make no mistake, these skills will shake the foundation of your entire life. After all, the quality of our relationships is directly influenced by how well or how badly we communicate. It can mean the difference between constant fighting and empowering conversation. Or the difference between a dull interaction and smooth-talking your way into a life-changing opportunity. Our only warning? We hope you're ready for these newfound abilities.

You see, communication is the closest thing to magic that exists. Once you master tone, language, timing, and a few other essential factors, you can produce any desired effect. The human mind is malleable, and except for the occasional idiosyncrasy, human needs are pretty easy to anticipate. Understanding them is the key to forming successful social strategies. You'll soon learn all about this.

I developed these advanced skills the hard way: through trial and error, through falling prey to the tactics of masters, and getting to know every personality type imaginable, no matter how aggravating. I studied the methods of a diverse range of people and learned from their mistakes as well as their successes. I said and did the wrong thing – but then I learned to say the right thing. And I perfected the right thing. I discovered when the right thing works best, when it doesn't work at all and when the right thing must give way to a better thing. I observed every move, every subtlety. And then I did extensive research to expand on what I already knew. I dissected the powerful areas of communication most people overlook; I will teach you to never overlook them again and how to use them to your fullest advantage.

I have watched fragile nobodies evolve into masters of persuasion with a presence that cannot be ignored. I am often thanked by people who have used my advice, with claims that it transformed their personal relationships, and helped them create new, more meaningful ones, as well. But it's no surprise that these benefits arise. Perfecting the art of conversation is synonymous with perfecting one's ability to live in tandem with other human beings. The people I've helped have become experts at both. I will be sharing these same secrets with you, very shortly.

With my help and expertise, you'll move past crippling shyness, dullness, and all breeds of social ineptitude. Instead, you'll spark fascinating interactions, deep connections and develop all the skills necessary to own every room you enter. You won't just open doors to new opportunities; you'll charm those doors right off their hinges. My guides will run the gamut, from seducing romantic interests to negotiating a better deal, children, difficult personalities, and more. You will need no other communication guide again. Consider this your conversation bible.

You've made that vital first step – now don't make the common mistake of ending the journey here. Remember this important fact: complacency is the silent killer of all potential. What doors are you allowing to shut while you sit idly?

As you reveal this book's next chapter, so shall you unveil *your* new chapter. Welcome to the only communication guide you'll ever need.

Chapter 1 - Establishing Likability

Imagine this: a man saunters into the party you're attending. He's dressed exceptionally well in a crisp, button-down shirt, smart casual pants, and polished leather shoes. He makes eye contact with everyone in the room for a brief moment, smiling occasionally, and gesturing a friendly hello to someone he recognizes. His body is open towards the room, and he's even nodding his head slightly to the rhythm of the music playing in the background. The woman you're talking to - your new acquaintance, Claire - notices him. She waves and beams, and he does the same. He looks between you both, surveying the situation, and then he comes over slowly, ready to introduce himself with a warm smile.

Before he's even said a word, this man has established himself as a likable person. There's a high likelihood that you already feel comfortable letting him join your conversation. You may even feel the desire to get to know him and consider him as a potential friend. It's true that you don't really know who he is, and it's possible he could be the opposite of what you expect – but the point is, you want to find out. And because he's displayed likable behavior, he's already at an advantage.

The Confirmation Bias

When we have a preexisting idea or belief, we tend to only notice factors that can confirm our assumptions. This idea forms the crux of the confirmation bias. In other words, you see what you want to see to confirm your initial judgment was correct. Humans enjoy being right. And so we absorb information selectively to prove our point, not disprove it.

How does this play into our scenario with the likable man? Let's say you finally speak to him, and he mistakenly assumes he's met you before and calls you by the wrong name. This would be a social flub on his part, but if you'd already established that you think he's likable, you'd probably let it slide easily. In fact, you'd probably think, "Oh, it's a simple mistake. It happens sometimes and you can't help it. I'm sure he meets a lot of people." You'd then forget it and instead choose to remember how kind he was when he apologized.

But consider this other scenario: let's say, it was a different man, and he walked into the room with a scowl and a tight jaw. When he looked around the room, his eyes lingered a bit too long and inappropriately on a good-looking woman, and when he noticed your friend, he raised his eyebrows and didn't smile. If the same occurrence happened where he called you by the wrong name, you probably wouldn't be so forgiving. You'd maybe think, "Clearly he doesn't really respect people." You would choose to remember the mistake he made, and even if he apologized, chances are you'd be harder to win over.

In both scenarios, you're only looking to confirm what you already believe – but you could be completely wrong about both assumptions. The first man could turn out to be an arrogant narcissist and the second man could turn out to be intelligent and kind, just very socially awkward. The problem is, we'd only know for sure if we sat down and got to know these men on a deeper level. But most social interactions don't grant us that much time and chances are, you've already decided you don't want to get to know the unlikable man.

This is why we must emphasize likable behavior. People are assessing whether they like or don't like you, and whether they want to get to know you or not, as soon as you walk in the room. And this will greatly influence all proceeding interactions. You may have a great personality, but no one will ever know about it if your behavior comes across as cold, awkward, or uninviting. Start off on the right foot and send positive signals.

The Qualities & Behaviors that Make You Instantly Likable

1. An Impressive Appearance

Contrary to popular belief, an impressive appearance doesn't just consist of good looks or expensive clothing. It encompasses everything about the way we carry and present ourselves to the world. It includes:

- <u>The way you dress</u>

Dressing well does not always mean formal. In fact, a necessary part of dressing well is making sure you've dressed appropriately for the occasion. If someone arrives at a low-key social gathering in a sharp suit for no reason, they may be perceived as pretentious. Conversely, if it's a formal event and you attend wearing sneakers, you'll be seen as sloppy and not taking it seriously.

People who dress sharply for every occasion (this means fitted, neat, and appropriate clothing) will always command more respect than someone who doesn't care at all about what they're wearing. Why? Not only does it send the message that you're intelligent and competent, it also tells people, "I am extremely socially aware and I have the means to take care of myself."

- <u>The way you speak</u>

Do you mumble or slur your words? Do you laugh nervously between sentences? Or do you enunciate and speak at just the right pace? The way you speak is a reflection of many important attributes. It will determine greatly how people perceive you and better yet, the way others will choose to interact with you. If your voice is too soft and slow, you will get overpowered. Studies have shown that those who display quiet voices give off the impression of being weak and inexperienced. At the opposite end, however, a voice that is high-pitched and loud is perceived to be unreliable, arrogant, and impatient.

The ideal voice is firm, well-defined, and at a medium pace and volume. Even if you're saying a simple greeting, project the voice that suits the message you want to send.

2. Open and Interested Body Language

Your gestures and stances are sending messages as well. You may not be aware of it, but every person who encounters you will respond to the positioning of your body. To enhance your likability, it's imperative that you display a sense of openness.

- <u>Turn towards the person you're speaking to</u>

Your face may be angled towards your conversation partner, but what about the rest of your body? When you're turned away, your body language could be interpreted as uninterested or nervous. Facing them squarely, however, will make you appear invested and interested in the conversation. This, in turn, will make people more inclined to engage with you.

- <u>Gesture with your hands or let your arms hang loose</u>

People tend to overlook what their arms are doing when they're conversing, but this is another tell-tale sign of how a person feels. Arms that are tight and locked give the impression of someone insecure or rigid. To appear more likable, let them hang loose and if you can, gesture as you speak. People tend to respond well to someone who is expressive with their hands. This will demonstrate that you're comfortable, confident and enthusiastic about the situation at hand.

- <u>Mirror your conversation partner's behavior</u>

Humans have a deep need to make connection with someone else. An effective way to ignite feelings of connection is to mimic someone's behavior in conversation. When they say something and smile, try smiling too. If they take a sip of their drink, you should as well. This will make the other party feel that you're in alignment with them, like you're on the same page. However, for mirroring to work successfully, it's important that you don't do it for the entire length of the conversation as this will seem unnatural and the other person will likely notice. Psychologists also advise not mirroring right away. If a conversation has not had time to find its rhythm, any conscious mimicry will be seen as such.

- Loose and upright posture

We all know that standing straighter conveys a more appealing impression, but that's not all there is to it. Our posture must also be fairly loose, as this tells people we're welcoming and comfortable. People who stand straight and rigidly tend to seem unapproachable and sometimes even severe.

3. Looking Happy to Be There

When a person looks happy to be where they are, they look comfortable and safe to be around. When we encounter someone who appears this way, we instinctively feel comfortable too, and we sense that their company must be pleasant. This is similar to displaying open body language, but not entirely the same. Open body language will say we're available, but a happy and pleasant aura will actually send the invitation.

- Smiling just the right amount

The most recognizable signal for happiness is the smile, and it's an easy way to convey your pleasure. Keep a relaxed smile on your face and you'll find that more people start interacting with you. Smile at the appropriate intervals when someone is telling a story and smile when you see someone that you know. Just be careful to not grin too much or too widely if it's not entirely genuine. A fake smile can be alarming and creepy, and may produce an adverse effect.

- Make sure your neutral expression is relaxed and pleasant

Many of us lose control of our neutral expressions. We think we look perfectly normal, but other people might still think we're unapproachable. Have you ever seen someone with Resting Bitch Face (RBF)? Exactly. Stay aware of what your neutral expression is. Even if you're just wandering over to the snack table to grab more finger food, keep your expression relaxed, with the corners of your mouth upturned ever so slightly. This is not a full on smile, but it conveys the message that you're happy to be there.

What Determines Likable Behavior?

Likable behavior is not made up of a random set of traits and actions, they can all be drawn down to the same basic needs. We search for basic assurances in every single person we encounter and this will determine how positively we respond to them as well as how likely we are to seek their company again. If you keep your conversation partners' three basic needs in mind, you may find yourself displaying likable behavior naturally.

- Safety

You may not realize this, but a number of qualities we search for, such as approachability and trustworthiness, can all be attributed to our desire for safety. The basic animal nature in us all wants to ensure that we'll receive no threats to our well-being. It's not just about our physical safety, but our sense of self as we know it. We want to avoid emotional and mental threats, just as we want to avoid a physical threat. When a person displays approachability or trustworthiness, they are essentially saying 'You're safe around me.' Once our brains pick up this signal, we relax and open ourselves to the possibility of connection.

- Significance

Once we establish we're safe, we soften to the idea of connecting, but we're not there immediately. We also want to feel significant and important on some level. It's not enough that a person is approachable. If they aren't really listening to what we're saying, or they're always looking over our shoulder cause they are waiting for an opportunity to talk to someone else, chances are we won't be entirely impressed. Even if someone is smiling and acting very kind, we can always sense when our presence is truly valued and desired. Naturally, we want to be where we are appreciated.

- Expansion

A new acquaintance has successfully made us feel comfortable and significant in their presence – but there's still something missing. The cherry on top of the cake is expansion and an opportunity for growth. The desire to evolve and become better than we are is a natural human need. The solution to this need can take many forms, but it all comes down to a feeling of excitement and positive challenge.

When we meet someone that entertains us and stimulates us intellectually, our need for mental and emotional expansion is fulfilled. This need also encompasses humor since what we find truly funny, subconsciously tickles our intellect. We've all encountered jokes that we consider "too dumb" or jokes we just "don't get."

This is the hardest need to take care of since personal taste can play a large role here. It is also important to note that people who can take care of each other's needs for expansion are usually from roughly the same IQ level. What one person finds interesting can be extremely boring or confusing to another person.

The Seven Bad Habits that are Making You Unlikable

Remember the unlikable guy from earlier? He's displaying a myriad of social turn-offs that are sending the wrong messages.

But do you want to know a terrifying thought? You, too, have definitely made some of those mistakes before. In fact, you might even make them to this day. Let's examine some classic and lesser known social mistakes, so you can start becoming more likable right now.

1. Constantly on the Phone

No one should feel bad for glancing at their phone or typing a quick text message, but in this modern day and age, such restraint is rare. If you have your phone out constantly, and are seen scrolling through social media while in the company of other people, you're going to leave a bad impression. Being absorbed by your device when other people expect you to stay present is seen as extremely rude. Would you start reading a book in the middle of a social gathering? Any decent person wouldn't, and this is not much different to frequent phone distractions. Save this behavior for when you're by yourself or at a very casual hang-out.

If you're expecting a call or trying to resolve something important via text, do so in another room. Or alternatively, apologize to the people you're with and explain how you're dealing with an important matter. This advice also applies to loud phone conversations in public. Find another room or lower your voice.

2. Slouching or Slumping in Your Seat

Unless you're at your best friend's house for a casual hang-out, slouching or slumping in your seat sends the signal that you're either lazy or submissive. To people you don't know, it can even convey a complete lack of interest in what they're saying. By slouching or slumping, you make your body appear smaller, and instinctively we interpret this as a lack of confidence and power.

3. Inappropriate or Lack of Eye Contact

Watching what someone does with their eyes is a great way to get a good read on them. Are they displaying judgment by looking everyone up and down? Are they being misogynistic by staring at women inappropriately? Or are they awkward and standoffish, making no eye contact at all? All of the above are examples of what can turn us off a new acquaintance. Avoid making those mistakes.

4. Bad Hygiene

When someone smells bad or looks like they haven't washed themselves in days, they're saying, "I can't take care of myself." As intelligent animals who are interested in self-preservation, we are wired to be repelled by something that we think is dirty. Subconsciously we associate it with breeding grounds for organisms and diseases that could threaten our well-being. Even if we know a person isn't diseased, the self-preserving animal in us has learned to have this reaction to potentially unsanitary situations, objects, or people.

Of course, no one stops caring for a friend or loved one because they have bad hygiene, but it is the reason we have the urge to hold our nose and sit further away from them. These reactions are not conducive to positive social interactions.

This reflex is hardwired into us in the same way we can't help but blink and produce tears when a foreign particle gets into our eyes. These are ways the living body has learned to cope with potential threats.

For this reason, most people (except for those who already live in unsanitary conditions) are repelled by bad hygiene. While it's perfectly normal to have a sweaty day now and then, where you may not smell as fresh as you usually do, consistent grime will make it difficult for you to charm anyone.

5. Not Participating in Conversations

Being mysterious is one thing, but if you are always seen staying completely silent in social settings, this can make you seem unfriendly or even dim-witted. When reserved people are in the presence of their outgoing friends, it comes naturally to let the talkers do the talking, but they should resist this urge. Even if it's just a one-liner or a question here and there, make sure you are contributing something to every conversation you're involved in. It's really quite simple: if you don't offer anything, you look like you have nothing to offer.

6. **Not Dressing Appropriately**

Remember what we said about dressing well for every occasion? Not everyone has a great sense of style, and that's okay, but at the very least, you must make sure you dress appropriately. This applies to men and women. Save your skimpy skirts and surfer tank tops for parties with your good friends, but never wear them to formal events or first-time meetings with your significant other's parents. Keep this in mind: always dress in alignment with the message you want to send to the room.

7. **Not Respecting Personal Space**

Personal space is more than just getting in someone's way or touching someone you don't know well. It encompasses behavior like cutting in front of a stranger in line, going through someone's belongings without permission, or entering someone's bedroom, office, or house without knocking first. Even actions that are intended to be friendly, like forcibly hugging someone you don't know, can be experienced as a violation of personal space. It depends on whether you were given verbal or nonverbal consent to enter someone's space or touch their property (and this includes their body).

Always respect the privacy of others, and their right to refuse physical contact. Anyone who witnesses such an invasion will see you as disrespectful and socially inept.

Never lose track of the way you present yourself to the world, whether physically or behaviorally. A conversation is far more than our verbal communications; it's also about what we say with our actions and responses. To truly master conversation skills, you must conquer the art of likable behavior.

Chapter 2 - The Basics of Good Conversation

You've learned how to behave in public, but the journey is far from over. As soon as you open your mouth to enter a conversation, you're in a different arena and a new set of skills comes into play. Our image is one thing, but as soon as this phase of communication begins, people finally get to see how that image stacks up against what we say and how we say it. Are we all that we portray ourselves to be? Are we as impressive as the words on our resume? Are we as classy as the way we dress?

How to Make Great First Impressions

You may think that short interactions are easier to pull off, but that could not be less true. Unlike sit-down chats or long conversations, you have a shorter amount of time to win the other party over. If you behave awkwardly or say something you shouldn't have, before you know it time's up, and that's how they'll remember you from now onwards. You have one try and then it's over until the next meeting, if it even exists.

Learning to master first impressions and small talk are crucial for many life-shaping events. A potential new employer doesn't have time or the interest to get to know you in depth, you need to charm him in a short amount of time. And the same rule applies to that cute boy or girl you run into sometimes. You need to make a good impression before you get that date.

To turn that one-time encounter into something more, here are some essential tips:

- **Butter up your introduction**

Don't just say 'My name is Peter,' say 'My name is Peter, it's really nice to meet you.' You'd be surprised by how simple a sentence can take your first impression up a few notches. This will immediately warm any new person to you, as you've successfully made them feel important, interesting, and like you want to continue being around them. We've established that humans enjoy feeling safe and significant; this is an easy, simple way to tick both those boxes immediately.

- **Learn how to give a good handshake**

Many potential employers and professional connections pay attention to the way you shake their hand. Keep in mind these three major factors: the strength of your grip, the duration, and the positioning of your hand.

The perfect handshake is not too soft, not too tight, but perfectly firm. You should shake their hand for two to three pumps, for no more than three seconds, but ideally two seconds. During the handshake, your arm should also be perfectly vertical. Never show the underside of your wrist or the top of your forearm, as this shows submission or dominance respectively.

Please note that if you shake hands with an individual who puts your hand on the bottom, with your wrist exposed, this means they are making a power play. If they pull you towards them as they shake your hand, they are also performing a power move. These are classic signs of exerting dominance. We don't advise making these power plays on other people, unless you are prepared for some tension.

- **Be considerate**

There's a good reason this encounter is brief. Perhaps you're talking to someone while they're at work, between meetings, or at a crowded social event. Whatever the scenario, be considerate of other peoples' time and attention. Consider the circumstances and question at what point you might become an intrusion. Are you trying to talk to someone while they're working? Or perhaps they're on their short lunch break and you're holding them up in the office corridor? Don't insist on holding a person's attention for a long time, when you know you're not the only reason they're there.

- **Make eye contact**

During quick encounters, many people shy away from eye contact. Whether it's due to social awkwardness or because you've been caught by surprise, resist the urge to let this discomfort be seen. Make sufficient eye contact with the person you're speaking with, but also resist the urge to stare. Look directly at them as they speak. For one-on-one conversations, you should break eye contact every 7-10 seconds. For group settings, however, try and break eye contact between 4-6 seconds.

- **Ask a question to show you're interested**

It's a quick chat, sure, but it's fine to shoot off a question as long as it's easy to answer and they aren't in a rush to get anywhere. This shows that you're interested and curious about them, since you chose to ask a question when you didn't have to. This is even more important for job interviews since employers expect questions, and will even judge prospective employees based on the questions they ask. Whatever the situation, make sure the questions you ask during brief encounters are not too personal or time-consuming.

- **Don't be *too* honest when you answer the question "How are you?"**

There are some individuals with which we *can* be honest about how we're doing – but they're all people we already know well, in which case, we are long past the stage of worrying about first-impressions. With the rest, however, it's best to keep it light and positive. Even if you're going through a difficult period in your life, understate it in a way that the other person doesn't suddenly feel they have to ask what's wrong and console you. Say something like, "I've been better, but I'm sure things will look up soon." Often when people ask you how you are, they're doing so out of politeness and good social decorum. Save your long, honest answers for your good friends and family. And always remember to ask the other person the same question!

- **Use environmental triggers**

If you can't think of a single thing to say, look around you. There's material everywhere! If you're running into someone at a grocery store, you could ask if they shop there often. If the encounter takes place at the train station, you could share where you're going and ask where they're headed as well. If the person in question is wearing something particularly striking, compliment them! Look around you in the moment and you'll realize there's a lot to talk about.

- **Give an uplifting goodbye**

Sometimes you get lucky and the person you've run into is someone you want to see again soon. You may make plans and part with a happy, "See you on Tuesday!" Most of the time, however, you're probably running into someone you don't care to see again, or someone you're not sure you'll see again, such as a prospective employer. To make the best impression, send them off with some positive and uplifting parting words. Tell them "Have a great day!" or give them well wishes in regards to what they've shared with you. For example, "Good luck with your marathon!" or "Have a great time at dinner!"

Win at Small Talk with the ARE Model

If you want a simple, easy formula for good small talk, this section is for you. Carol Fleming, a communications expert and coach, created a three-point method for helping individuals get better at small-talk. This plan works on shy and confident folks alike. ARE stands for:

- **Anchor** – To begin, find something that you are your conversation partner both have in common in the current moment. Fleming describes this as your "shared reality." Look around and see what you notice. It could be anything from the food being served or someone in an outrageous outfit that you can both see. Anchoring involves choosing a focus and stating the observation. For example, let's say you're making small talk at a fancy party. You tell a new acquaintance: "These appetizers are delicious."

- **Reveal** – Then comes something about you. Share a slightly personal tidbit that's relevant to the topic you've just brought up. It doesn't have to be complicated or mind-blowing. This is just to establish the dynamic of sharing with each other. You could say, "I wish I could make something like this, but I'm just not very skilled in the kitchen."

- **Encourage** – Finally, you give your acquaintance an opening to respond. Focus on being friendly and encouraging so that they share information about themselves with you. This should take the form of a question. An idea is: "Are you a good cook? You look like someone with a lot of hidden talents!"

Whenever you're feeling nervous or more unsteady than usual, remember this formula to get yourself back into the small-talk groove. Don't shy away from small talk. It's the precursor to a long, engaging conversation with a potential new friend or professional connection. It is the first step that leads to all other steps. Keep these tools in mind to start winning at small talk.

Three Essential Ways to Get Along with Anyone You Meet

We all know someone with seemingly irresistible charm; someone who's liked by everyone they meet, no matter the personality type and no matter the circumstance. The trick to getting along with others is not rocket science, but it does require a big mental and behavioral shift. We might have already displayed likable behavior, earning the interest of a new conversation partner, but now we need to know how to sustain this interest. Now that someone has given us the chance to get to know them, we need a new set of skills to create conversational harmony.

1. Show Genuine Interest in Others

It seems simple, doesn't it? And yet you'd be surprised by how many fail this basic step. Showing genuine interest requires more than just nodding and smiling. Remember the basic social need for significance? The person you're conversing with must feel that you care about what they're saying and who they are. We all want to feel as though we are valued and appreciated. These behaviors can demonstrate genuine interest:

- Ask questions. Get to know the person you're conversing with better, but make sure to do so in a way that is not interrogative, and steer clear of questions that are too personal unless you know them well. If they are telling you about an activity they enjoy, ask them why they like it, or when they started.

- Pay attention. When someone is talking, stay present and listen to what they're saying. Most people can sense when the person they're talking to has zoned out of the conversation, and this is a major social turn off. Why would you want to talk to someone who isn't listening? You wouldn't. If someone is telling a story, try to paint a mental picture with the details they're giving you. A good trick is to imagine what they're saying as a movie.

- Show enthusiasm. When someone talks to you, don't just nod and blink like a fool. Smile, look receptive, and when they share new information with you, show enthusiasm. When necessary, respond with phrases like, "Wow, that's very interesting!" or "How wonderful. That's great to hear." People always respond well to enthusiastic positivity.

2. Be Kind

People who display kindness are pleasant to be around: that's a fact. We instinctively feel safe around them and develop trust for them. An act or word of kindness can easily brighten up a day, and it's an important step to getting along with someone. You'll be hard pressed to find someone who isn't won over by kindness. Here are some ideas for showing your nice side:

- Display good manners. That's right, everything your parents taught you about saying please and thank you, holding open the door, respecting personal space, and all the rest, are all valuable social skills. Manners display consideration for other people. The reason we are taught this when we are young is because this is the most basic form of human kindness. Display good manners and you'll start off on the right foot.

- Empathize. This doesn't mean you have to listen to someone's problems and hold their hand; we can always empathize, even over small matters. Perhaps, you're at a formal dinner and someone's food gets forgotten. Say something like, "I'm so sorry you have to wait. It's always annoying when food doesn't arrive on time." It's simple, but filled with empathy. The other person will immediately feel like you care about them, and will be highly receptive to anything else you might say.

3. Open Up

Remember our need for expansion? It's not enough to be kind and receptive, we should also show our conversation partners that we have something to offer them. We do this by opening up, talking about ourselves, and responding to what they say in a thoughtful, informative or entertaining manner.

- Share your experiences. The best part of this is it can be anything that delights you to share. The only requirements are that it is appropriate and doesn't dominate the entire conversation for an extended period of time. You can share anything, from a funny encounter you had that day to a fascinating experience you had abroad. Keep it interesting and leave out the unnecessary details. When we share stories with others, it allows them to get to know us and invites them to see what is interesting about us.

- Share an interesting thought, feeling, or observation. If you don't have any relevant experiences to share, or you simply can't think of anything, then try to respond to your current surroundings or the conversation at hand. Ideally, it would be something that reflects your personal taste or an opinion you hold. They want to get to know you, remember?

Six Tips for Resisting Shyness and a Lack of Confidence

Some of you can't help it – you're shy, and that's just the way you are. You're more wary of people, and you've never understood how chatterboxes can so freely interact with others they don't know. Even if you have the desire to socialize, you end up not contributing very much to the conversation. Sometimes this is because you have social anxiety and a lack of confidence, and other times, it's just because you're more reserved than the average person.

There's nothing wrong with being shy or reserved, but you'll definitely encounter situations in your life where you'll need to talk more than you're comfortable with. Perhaps you're talking to a prospective employer, or maybe you're meeting a significant other's parents for the first time. To safeguard against awkward moments and silences, keep these tips in mind:

1. Prepare beforehand

If you're nervous about an upcoming social interaction, there's nothing wrong with preparing for it in advance. Think of interesting stories to tell, and perhaps even practice the way you want to tell them. If you're feeling confident, prepare some jokes. Make sure you know them well but try not to over-rehease, or they won't sound natural.

If you already know about potential conversation topics that the other person will bring up, it's also a great idea to think of how you will respond. For example, if you're about to spend time with someone who recently did a lot of traveling, think of an interesting travel experience that you've had, and practice telling the story in an amusing way. Use what you know about the people you're spending time with to come up with great conversation topics and stories.

If you're about to meet your significant other's parents for the first time, and you know they'll ask you about your career or where you grew up, think of engaging and relevant stories that you can share with them. To be extra prepared, come up with a list of questions to ask whenever there is a lull in the conversation.

Planned interactions can turn out extremely well, and the best part is, you'll feel a lot more confident afterwards.

2. Focus away from yourself

If you dread being the center of attention, this is a tip for you. There are many ways to direct the spotlight onto someone else. One sure way is to ask lots of questions. Instead of staying silent, try to learn about someone else. This will reflect upon you positively as you'll also appear curious and interested, two qualities that people tend to be drawn to. You won't have to feel vulnerable, and yet you're still participating in the conversation.

To keep attention off yourself for as long as possible, make sure to ask open-ended questions, not just something that can be answered with a 'yes' or 'no.' If you meet someone from a foreign place, ask them what it's like where they are from, and if you're speaking with a work acquaintance, ask them what they like to do on the weekends. To successfully avoid the spotlight, think of more questions to keep the conversation evolving. Otherwise, the other person will likely ask "How about you?" if silence presents itself.

3. Focus on connecting, not impressing

During moments of anxiety, people tend to forget that it's more important to connect than it is to impress. If you focus on impressing, you'll most likely come across as trying too hard and making all the wrong moves. People can sense when someone is actively trying to impress, and this tends to produce a negative reaction. What you should focus on is genuine connection. Get to know the other person, empathize with them, and don't be afraid to give them a genuine compliment. Instead of thinking about all the ways you can show off, really listen to what they're saying and respond in a thoughtful manner. Try to also discover your common interests.

4. Don't be someone you're not

Shy people should never forget this fact. In the pursuit of better conversation skills, it can be easy to feel like you're trying to be someone else, but it's important to remember it's not like that at all. It's not about giving yourself qualities that you don't have, it's about developing enough confidence to share the qualities you possess with other people. Shy people should never feel the need to pretend they're extroverted or gregarious people. It's about getting used to including your great qualities and interesting experiences in the wider conversation.

There are many ways that people pretend to be someone they are not. Sometimes this manifests in false stories and lies, and sometimes even fake personas and forced behavior. If you find yourself doing this, your attempt at socializing will backfire. Fake people attract other fake people, and this will repel meaningful connections.

5. Recognize that you have something to contribute

We've all lived unique lives and we need to recognize there's something about all of us that makes us interesting. No one has lived exactly the same life as you. You may share the same hometown, the same parents, or even a similar trauma to someone else, but no one possesses the same combination of upbringing, experiences, and choices as you. This means you're unique and you have something to contribute that no one has ever heard before. You need to recognize that you have valuable insights. You may feel shy or reserved, but consider the fact that other people in the conversation might benefit from hearing your point of view.

6. Understand that not everyone is as confident as they seem

You're not alone. Chances are high that even the person you're talking to is fighting their shier urges. While there certainly are many extroverted and socially comfortable people out there, the majority of people identify as an introvert. Even wildly successful individuals like Mark Zuckerberg and Steven Spielberg are known to have shy and anxious tendencies. Yet you'd never guess it with the number of public appearances they've both made and, most importantly, with how confident they come across. Know that you, too, can seem this confident, even if you don't feel that way deep down inside.

Chapter 3 - Igniting Exceptional Interactions

You've made it past first impressions and you've pulled them into a full on conversation. Now what? At this point, many people find themselves at a loss for words, unsure of what exactly to say next. You've already asked them how they've been, what they did over the summer, and told them how great their outfit is. Now, they're looking at you expectantly and you have no idea how to fill the silence.

We all crave engaging discussions and a genuine bond, but when you're standing in that silence, it can feel impossible. How can we make what we say mean something? What can we do to break away from hum-drum hellos and how-do-you-dos? How can we be interesting conversationalists?

Conversation Topics & Tips for Every Possible Scenario

Depending on the exact circumstances, certain topics may be more or less appropriate for the occasion. Nevertheless, there are a great deal of topics that can ignite fascinating discussion, regardless of context.

For the most successful delivery, it's advised to work in new topics as naturally as possible instead of simply blurting out a question. For best results, try and include an interesting story or observation that is relevant to the topic.

Friends

We should feel comfortable around our friends, but there are many scenarios in which we might not. For example, with new friends. Or perhaps, if you're talking one-on-one with a friend that you normally see with a group. Dynamics also change depending on how many people are involved, and it's wise to adjust communication methods to the exact context.

With groups, it's a good idea to ask questions that give everyone the opportunity to contribute and share. Asking overly personal questions in a group setting may make someone feel put on the spot, and it's likely the whole group doesn't want to slow down to listen to one person's story for a long time. Keep questions, in these scenarios, open to everyone.

When you're in a one-on-one talk, on the other hand, conversation can be highly engaging if you ask them questions you wouldn't normally ask. Take a look at these examples for some ideas:

New Friends

- How long have you known each other and how did you meet?
- What does everyone think about that latest episode in [insert TV show here]?
- What did everyone do last weekend?
- Does anyone have any funny bad date stories?
- What is everyone binging on Netflix right now?
- What's the craziest thing you've seen on the news recently?
- Has anyone here ever met a celebrity? If so, what happened?
- What's the most trouble you've ever gotten into?
- If your life story was turned into a movie and this moment made it into a scene, who would play you and who would you choose to play everyone else?
- How would you say you've changed since High School?

One-on-One Conversations

- How is work going?
- Are you seeing anyone these days?
- What do you think of [random mutual friend]'s new girlfriend/boyfriend?
- How often do you see your family?
- What's the most embarrassing thing that's ever happened to you?

- Do you consider yourself an introvert or an extrovert?
- How many relationships have you had and which one shaped you the most?
- What's the worst sexual experience you've ever had?
- What are some goals you're currently trying to achieve?
- Have you ever gotten into a physical fight?
- Which world cultures are you most fascinated by?

Work Acquaintances

There will be a range of intimacy levels with work acquaintances. Some you may be very comfortable with while others feel distant. Regardless of how well you get along, it's always best to keep conversations with colleagues somewhat professional. This doesn't mean that all talks need to be stiff and formal, it simply means they should remain within a narrow realm of topics. With the exception of rare circumstances, questions that are personal will not be seen as appropriate.

- If you didn't have this job, what would you be doing instead?
- What do you like to do on the weekends?
- How do you recharge after a long workday?
- Do you have any tricks for making it through a stressful workday?
- What's the weirdest job you've ever had?
- Have you ever had a crush on a coworker?
- If you could have lunch with anyone in the world, who would it be?

Family

Unlike our friends and romantic partners, we don't choose our family. And shared DNA doesn't always mean shared interests. It's not uncommon for family time to be awkward. Whether it's your family or someone else's family you're spending time with, one thing is for sure: family topics are always welcome. A great conversation starter is to ask about a specific family story, or question them about their earlier family life. This can spark a fascinating story and the chosen family member will feel touched by your curiosity.

<u>Your Family</u>

- Do we have any precious family heirlooms?
- What's our ancestry?
- What was your favorite pastime when you were a child?
- Do we have any interesting family secrets that I don't know about?
- Are we related to anyone famous?
- Who do you think I'm the most similar to in our family?
- What are some dominant familial traits?
- What's the most awkward moment you've ever seen at a family gathering?
- What was the first job you ever had?
- What are some of the biggest ways the world has changed since you were younger?
- What was [random family member] like when he/she was younger?
- How did [married family members] meet? (also feel free to ask this question directly to the subjects)

Romantic

There is a little more wiggle room when it comes to conversations with a romantic interest. This is because both parties are often actively trying to get to know each other, so questions that would normally seem out-of-the-blue are not that unusual. For example, if you're talking to a regular acquaintance and ask them, "How long was your longest relationship?" they may consider this question very personal and nosey. But on a date with a romantic interest, getting to know each other is expected. After all, you are trying to test how compatible you are.

- What are your guilty pleasures?
- Are you close with your family?
- Are you more like your mother or your father?
- What were you like as a teenager?
- How long was your longest relationship?
- How do you think you've changed in the last 10 years?
- What's your love language?
- Do you prefer fun nights out or cozy nights in?
- If you could settle down in any country in the world, which one would you choose?
- What's a movie, song, or book that has really shaped the way you see the world?
- What's your weirdest or most interesting habit?
- What's your favorite way to experience nature?
- What's your dream job?
- Who are your best friends and why?
- Do you consider yourself an introvert or an extrovert?
- What was the most challenging aspect of your childhood?
- How comfortable are you with public displays of affection?
- What would you consider a deal-breaker in a relationship or potential partner?

The Worst Mistakes You Can Make in a Conversation

Once we begin actively talking to someone, there are many reasons the interaction could fall flat. It's not always for the reason you think and chances are, even though you think you're socially adept, you're making at least one of these mistakes.

1. **Talking about yourself too much**

If you come across as a narcissist, you can say goodbye to a genuine human connection. While people may enjoy learning about you, you shouldn't expect them to listen to long stories about your life without asking for theirs in return. It takes two to form a connection, and if there's no space for another person in the conversation, what's the point? If you notice yourself continuously changing the subject to you and your life, stop and ask your conversation partner something about their life. Listen carefully while they tell their story, and do not respond with something about yourself each time. Instead, try to acknowledge what they've said and extend understanding or an observation.

2. Acting like a know-it-all

Due to our need for expansion, we enjoy being around smart people. We don't, however, enjoy being around know-it-alls. You may be wondering what the difference is, and the answer is simple: know-it-alls are smart people who constantly feel the need to prove they're smart. Do you go on long tangents, explaining complex or obscure ideas to people who don't care and didn't ask for an explanation? Do you go out of your way to demonstrate your breadth of knowledge because you want recognition? You might be a know-it-all. This can be another form of narcissism but occasionally, it can signify a lack of-self esteem. Know-it-alls are sometimes so insecure that they latch onto the one trait they feel confident about, their intelligence. If this sounds like you, resist the urge to prove how smart you are all the time. This will only push people away. After all, if you're acting above them, how can they form a connection with you?

3. Being pedantic

Pedantry can sometimes signify a know-it-all, but not all the time. Even unintelligent people can be pedantic. What makes a pedant? Someone who is overly concerned with unimportant details and rules. They will go out of their way to correct people about trivial facts, even if it has no bearing on the conversation.

Let's say you're telling a new acquaintance about something amusing that happened to you and your friend, Rhonda, who is also present.

"We were just at a restaurant on 3rd and Geary Street," you begin to say, "And a woman asked for my autograph. Turns out she mistook me for a celebrity!"

You and your new acquaintance laugh, but Rhonda says, "Actually, the restaurant was on 3rd and Brady, not Geary." In this scenario, Rhonda is being pedantic. This detail is not important to the story, but she had to chime in anyway. After this comment, there is likely to be an awkward pause in the conversation. Don't interrupt the good mood for an insignificant detail. Avoid the urge to correct people if it makes no difference to the conversation. Let it go!

4. Oversharing

We all want to form an emotional connection. Intimate friendships or relationships can be great catalysts for this. When you share information that is too personal with someone you are not close to, however, this is called oversharing. Let's turn to socially awkward Rhonda again. She's meeting up with a new friend for the first time and they're having a casual lunch in town. She realizes that it's Monday the 3rd, and she suddenly remembers that her parents got divorced on Monday the 3rd many years ago. She begins telling her new friend all about the trauma she endured when her parents became divorced.

The new friend has just been on the receiving end of oversharing. Rhonda doesn't know her new friend that well yet, and she has already started sharing something extremely personal. This puts the other party in an uncomfortable place because they are still casually getting to know you, but now they feel they need to console you. Save your personal stories for after you know a person reasonably well.

5. Being pretentious

Pretentiousness is very common, and we're all guilty of it sometimes. We can be pretentious for many reasons. Perhaps, we want to look more cultured, more popular, or just generally more interesting. A know-it-all can also be classified as being pretentious if their intention is to impress someone. A pretentious person tends to enjoy showing off and exaggerating some aspect of themselves. They may want to impress people by demonstrating they've read obscure books that most people don't understand, or perhaps they are constantly name-dropping famous people they've met to seem more influential. Whatever it is they're trying to demonstrate, no one likes a pretentious person. This is because pretentious people are playing a game, and others can sense it. Since people respond more positively to honesty and sincerity, pretentiousness can ruin your chances at getting someone to like you.

6. Not paying attention

We've all met someone like this. Sometimes they are narcissists who can't stop talking about themselves, but other times they may just appear disinterested and distracted. However it manifests, we've all had a conversation with someone who doesn't seem to be listening to what we're saying. It seems as if they're only waiting for their chance to respond. Not listening to our conversation partner is a major social faux pas. The other person can always tell and even if they don't show it, it's probably annoying them.

7. Preaching and lecturing

We tend to associate this kind of behavior with our parents or teachers – if you don't want your new friends to think of you as a nagging and annoying presence, then stay away from all forms of preaching and lecturing. Judgmental people can be prone to this kind of behavior, but other times it can be the result of attempted helpfulness gone wrong. It occurs when one party feels they know the best course of action on a particular subject, and instead of talking to their peers about it as an equal, they end up talking *at* them. Someone who engages in this behavior will constantly try to tell people what they 'should' do, and ramble on in the same way a parent does.

If you disagree with something an acquaintance or friend did, try asking questions to incite reflection. Or perhaps share a similar experience that you've had or heard of, and explain what the consequences were. Do this in a gentle and compassionate manner. There are many ways to make a suggestion without preaching.

8. Being easy to offend

The modern day has opened up many important conversations about the way we treat each other. Some people, however, have taken this a little too far. They insist on being offended even by minor things and will go out of their way to shove blame on anyone. If it's clear that no harm was intended, chill out and let it go. If someone says something ignorant out of a lack of knowledge instead of nastiness, gently enlighten them and then move on. People who are easily offended or upset cause others to feel as though they are walking on eggshells. And guess what? No one wants to talk to a person that makes them feel this way.

9. Talking badly about other people

It's a cheap trick to try and bond with someone. You don't know what else to talk about, so you try to connect with someone over mutual dislike for others. Sometimes it can even be a backwards way of complimenting the person you're talking to. For example, "You have such a beautiful home! Have you been to Jessica's house? Her decor is *so* tacky. And Kate's house is a total mess. You definitely have the nicest home of all." Unfortunately, this does work on some people, but this behavior is commonly associated with teenagers and high school politics. Friends who take on this dynamic encourage the worst parts of each others' personalities.

If you're looking to create a healthy connection that truly enriches your life, we don't advise talking badly about other people. Mature, secure, and emotionally stable individuals will immediately be repulsed by such behavior. If you are willing to talk this way about other people you know, there's little stopping you from talking this way about them.

Ideas to Steer Clear of Boring Conversations

Let's start off with a hard truth: some boring conversations cannot be prevented. Why? Because it takes more than one person to make it interesting. You can say all the right things and pull out the most effective techniques, but if the other person is obstinate and closed-off, then you can't control their behavior.

The good news is these instances are a rarity. Most shy and serious people can be pulled out of their shell with the right coaxing. Truth is, everyone has a humorous, interesting, or unusual side to them – you just have to find out how to access it.

1. Share an embarrassing or unusual story

Conversations become boring when no one is taking any risks. No one is sharing anything new, they're just saying what they feel they are supposed to say. When someone shares a genuine thought, feeling or observation, however, you'll notice your mind waking up. We are wired to find truth and honesty interesting, because it's something we can all connect with. It sends a signal that we can be ourselves. If you want to open up a new acquaintance and get them to expose a side of their personality they don't show anyone, you must create a safe environment for them. A great way to get the ball rolling is to share a story of your own. If it makes you seem a little vulnerable, they'll be far more engaged and likely to share something similar with you.

2. Identify passions and ask about them

It's a no-brainer: everyone loves to talk about what they're passionate about. Listen out for what people say they enjoy and ask them for more details once you learn what it is. This might be someone's job, but not always since a lot of people don't really enjoy their jobs. To find out what these passions could be, pay attention to what people said they did on the weekends or don't be shy, just ask them what their favorite hobbies are!

3. Ask an open-ended question

You are completely within power to redirect the course of a conversation if you so desire. A great way to do this is by asking questions. Stay away from 'yes' or 'no' questions, however, since this will give people the opportunity to give a short answer. An open-ended question will force them to elaborate and take their answer to a more interesting place. Since they'll have to think more about their answer, they'll be more engaged in the conversation. Instead of the question "Do you enjoy your new job?" try asking "What is it like at your new job and what do you enjoy about it?" If all else fails, ask for their honest opinion on something.

4. Respond genuinely and elaborately

We've already established that people respond to honesty. That's why you should always respond to people genuinely, and without any pretenses. Please note that this is different from being brutally honest, where we may share an inappropriate or hurtful truth. Being genuine simply means we are not trying to be someone we are not. When we speak elaborately, we give the other person more to respond to.

5. Embrace your silly side

In other words, tell a joke every now and then. Bring some humor into the way you speak. Just keep it appropriate and mature, avoiding all humor that degrades another person. Silliness does not just mean silly faces or pranks (avoid this unless you're with good friends!) it means infusing a sense of the ridiculous into your conversation.

6. Lighten up

We all want to avoid boring conversations, but listen, don't stress yourself out. Chances are your conversation partners can tell when you're trying extremely hard. It may even manifest in over-seriousness or too much intensity which can put people off. Part of the trick is to just take it easy and enjoy yourself. Lighten up. Keep all these tips in mind but be natural and exude positivity, no matter how the conversation is going.

Three General Rules for Sparking an Interesting Conversation

1. Bring up something *you* find interesting

One way we tend to sabotage a conversation is by only bringing up the topics we feel we're supposed to bring up. We stick to safe topics because we think that's what's expected of us. Unfortunately, this is a pretty common formula for a boring conversation – and why would you expect anything more than that? After all, even you don't really care about these topics, do you? To truly make a conversation interesting, bring up a topic you're actually fascinated by. There's a good chance that if you find it engaging, the other person will too.

2. Deepen conversation topics over time

It's completely normal to start off with a lighthearted topic. We all need to ease in. However, we can always make our conversations more interesting by taking them to a deeper level. And don't be scared of the word 'deep.' It doesn't mean you need to talk about existentialism or traumatic heartbreak. It just means that you need to get to the core of the subject and make it completely relatable.

For example, let's say two people start off talking about their cats and all the funny, adorable habits their little feline friends have. If they just stick to this aspect of their cats, they'll eventually run out of things to say. To keep things interesting, they need to take the topic to new depths. They should tell the stories of how they found their cats, complete with the emotions of it all, and they should discuss how it is that their cats bring so much to their lives. They could ponder interesting questions about pet-owner relationships, or what unique benefits a cat brings and a dog doesn't. Deepening a topic creates a bond. Try it in your next conversation.

3. Be as specific as possible

Speaking in vague and general terms is a sure way to bore and frustrate your conversation partner. If someone asks you what you like to do on the weekends, don't just say, "I like to go out with friends." Give a more complete answer. When we offer up generalities, it doesn't give our conversation partners any material to respond to. This can result in awkwardness or strained conversation. It also sends the message that you're not very enthusiastic about the conversation at hand.

Instead of the above statement, say something more detailed like, "I like to go out with friends. We enjoy nightclub-hopping on the weekends and when that gets too much, we like to take road trips out into nature." The amended statement opens up two new doors: nightclubs and nature. Always aim to open new doors with your responses. Make it easy on your new acquaintances!

Chapter 4 - Cultivating Charisma and Magnetism

It's one thing to have pleasurable conversations every now and then, but what if you want more than that? Some of us are blessed with charisma and magnetism. This means you don't have to pursue interesting interactions and people, instead they seem to find you. A small portion of people are gifted and naturally magnetic, but the rest of us shouldn't give up hope. Like most things in life, you don't have to be gifted to be good at something. You just need the self-awareness, knowledge, and the practice.

We've all met someone with charisma and magnetism. People are drawn to them like moths to light, purely because their presence is energizing and enjoyable. Magnetic individuals take communication skills to a new level entirely. They know which rules should be followed strictly, which ones should be broken, and which ones are exceptions in certain circumstances.

Magnetic individuals find it easier than most to achieve career success, large friend groups, and a wide variety of romantic options. The development of these qualities is no easy feat, but it can be done. First, however, you need to know the secrets.

The Thirteen Secrets to Developing a Magnetic Personality

1. **Cultivate emotional self-sufficiency**

Arguably one of the most powerful qualities to develop, emotional self-sufficiency is a major driving force behind magnetic individuals. Quite simply, it signifies an ability to monitor your own emotions and needs, and understand exactly how to satisfy them without outside help. There is no dependence on other people to take care of their needs because they know how to do it themselves. They have mastered the teaching of 'You cannot control other people's actions, only your reactions' and they live closely by it. They focus on what they can control and nothing more. Other people are drawn to this quality because it makes a person seem stable, secure, and smart. We tend to trust someone who has control over their emotions as it gives the impression of maturity.

2. Your presence must give just as much as it takes

A truly magnetic personality does not operate from a 'me, me, me' philosophy. In fact, they make sure that other people in the conversation get something they need as well. Sometimes it's empathy, encouragement, gentle honesty, or even recognition. They are not afraid to compliment others, and when they do, it comes from a genuine place, instead of just wanting to score points. They might share interesting stories about themselves, but more than this, they are curious about other people, they ask questions, and they share comments that are both helpful and authentic. When people benefit from an interaction with you, whether it's mentally or emotionally, they are far more likely to seek your company again.

3. Learn to balance intelligence, humor and kindness

These three qualities are some of the most difficult to learn but when used in tandem, they can be irresistible. Intelligence allows us access to a large pool of data, humor makes it fun, and kindness creates the bond. People with strong magnetism utilize this trifecta to their advantage and with it, they charm people instantly.

4. Don't be afraid of vulnerability

Many people make the mistake of coming across too tough and impervious. Contrary to popular belief, this is not a good way to attract interesting connections. While it may temporarily impress or even intimidate people, it won't make anyone crave your company. This is because machismo or toughness is a pretense, and it will only attract people putting on the same pretense. Magnetic people are not afraid of being vulnerable. If it's relevant and appropriate, they have no issue sharing a heartfelt comment or allowing someone a glimpse into their true feelings. They do so in a manner that does not seek attention or overshare. People are drawn to this because we are engaged by sincerity.

5. Learn how to read people like a book

It takes more than one person to create a successful social interaction. This is why a great communicator doesn't just focus on their own behavior, they also notice how others behave. They are masters at reading and interpreting signals to determine the mood of anyone around them. This skill is important because a person's mood can change constantly, and it will shape the way they perceive the world. This means that a persuasion tactic that works on happy Person A might not work on anxious Person B. Using what they gather from observation, magnetic people are able to adjust their tactics and behavior so as to elicit any desired response from anyone.

6. Stop publicizing everything

Magnetic people value privacy greatly, and you may even find that some of them carry an air of mystery. Do not try to become intentionally mysterious, as this is likely to backfire. Instead, learn to hold certain memories and experiences as sacred. Learn to see the value in privacy and stop publicizing everything about your life. Share deeply personal matters with a select few and resist blabbermouth tendencies. Someone who shares personal details incessantly comes across as overly-emotional and as having no control. These are qualities that tend to repel people instead of attracting them.

7. Learn to adapt

This valuable skill can only be learned through experience and trial-and-error. Once gained however, it will get you far. Magnetic individuals can adapt to a range of different scenarios and can get along with many kinds of people. Men, women, young, old, and even people from other cultures. They can pick up on the rhythm and communication style of their conversation partner, the type of stories they value, and they can adjust their behavior accordingly. At the end of the day, they know that whoever it is, you can always connect to the aspects of humanity that we all have in common.

8. Make the best of what makes you different

While there are certain social codes that are absolutely necessary, magnetic individuals are not fussed about total conformity. As long as they're dressed well and appropriately, they see no reason why they should wear the exact same style as everyone else. As long as they're being polite and considerate, why should they stick to the same humdrum conversation topics that everyone else is discussing? Magnetic people won't go out of their way to stand out from a crowd, but they will embrace their natural eccentricities and proclivities.

9. Stop feeling embarrassed about every misstep

There are certain situations in which shame and embarrassment are deserved. For instance, if something mean we've said or something unethical we have done is exposed, then we should feel shame for those actions. But if no harm has been done or intended, a magnetic person rejects feelings of embarrassment. Why? Because, at the end of the day, only we can embarrass ourselves.

Perhaps, you showed up to a party and are wearing the exact same outfit as another person. Consider these two opposite ways of reacting to this scenario:

- You sink into the nearest armchair and hope no one notices you. You immediately start telling your friend, "I can't believe it! I need to leave or find a new outfit." As you talk, you and your friend continue to look at this person, and they notice.

Your face turns red, and everything about your body language says you don't want to be seen. The other party attendees notice the similar clothes, and since you are noticeably embarrassed, they are embarrassed for you. It affects your interactions for the rest of the night, as people are turned off by your awkward behavior.

- You notice the person in the same clothes and can't help but see the amusement in the situation. What are the odds? You go up to the other person and say jokingly, "Can I just say you have a fantastic sense of style?" You both laugh, and so do the people around you. It is no longer an awkward situation because you have made light of it. The party attendees respect you for being able to laugh at yourself. Since everyone has seen what a great sense of humor you have, people want to converse and joke around with you for the rest of the night. After a while, no one even thinks about the similar clothes.

The moral of the story is: the only difference between people laughing *at* you and laughing *with* you, is that you're not laughing as well. If you choose to see the humor in your 'embarrassing' moments, you can never be humiliated.

See the absurdity in every situation and always continue to have a good time. Ask yourself, "What difference does this make in the grand scheme of my life?" The answer is likely, "No difference at all."

10. Realize there's something to learn from everyone

There's no such thing as truly boring people. Everyone is interesting if you get to know them, and everyone has something to contribute. Magnetic people recognize this. In a new crowd, they stay aware of everyone's unique and positive qualities and they learn from them, when possible. Pay attention to what makes your acquaintances different and use that to hone in what you could learn from them. It could be anything from an effective negotiation strategy or a comedic sensibility to unique stories about a faraway culture or a complex industry you know nothing about. Stay open to learning and allow others to teach you.

11. Don't be afraid to say you don't know

When we encounter a topic that we don't understand, many feel the need to pretend to know more than they do. This can suffice for quick encounters when there's not much time to chat, but at all other times, one should never feel ashamed of saying, "That's interesting, I never knew that."

Let's say, you're talking at length with someone and they start bringing up the economy, it's possible that this is a topic you don't know much about. Have the confidence to say, "This sounds fascinating. Tell me more about how it works." You can even use this opportunity to compliment and get to know someone. You could say, "I wish I knew more about this, but I never took time to learn. How did you become so knowledgeable?" We tend to trust people who are open about their shortcomings, as it makes them seem humble, self-aware and comfortable with who they are. It allows us to let our guard down. Furthermore, when we give someone the opportunity to feel like they can teach us something, it makes them feel significant and interesting.

12. Do not give any attention to someone who doesn't respect you

We've established that magnetic people are intelligent and empathic, but a necessary quality is also self-respect. You can be kind, complimentary, and try your best to get to know someone, but if they begin behaving rudely, you must drop that social interaction like a hot potato. If you allow someone to disrespect you, then other people will realize they can get away with this behavior. It sends a signal that you have no self-respect and will put up with abuse. Distance yourself from anyone that disrespects you and if you can't, then it's time to brush up on your classy comebacks.

13. Build a large network of diverse connections

It can be tempting to only connect or befriend people from your industry of work, but this isn't the way of a magnetic person. Include a diverse range of people in your social circle. Open yourself up to individuals from other cultures, genders, sexual orientations, religions, work industries, and more. Not only can it feel fulfilling to have a large group of friends, but you'll come across as multi-faceted and well-connected.

All You Need to Know About the Trifecta of Charm

The trifecta of charm consists of intelligence, humor, and empathy. When combined in the right way, this formidable combination of qualities can charm almost anyone. In some cases, it can even override your physical appearance, making you come across as attractive even if you are not conventionally so. While most people embody at least one of these traits, they must work together to produce the best results.

In a conversation, intelligence alone makes one seem stiff and inaccessible, while someone gifted with only humor will come off too childish and silly. Empathy is a valuable trait, but without intelligence or humor it creates an individual that is too soft and overly emotional. The trifecta of charm utilizes all three at once and in equal measure.

Unfortunately, these qualities are also some of the most difficult to teach. In order to develop them, individuals must work hard at assimilating new habits into their personality, and must engage in a significant amount of study. Some trial-and-error may be necessary, and personal style will vary with each person. Still, it is absolutely possible for someone who scores low on all three counts to add the trifecta of charm to their social arsenal. They need only follow these tips:

- **Intelligence**

Intelligence can be described in a number of different ways, but at its core, it's comprised of several basic functions. Problem-solving, reasoning, logic, and critical thinking are some of the most notable. Many believe you're either intelligent or you're not, but this has proven to be far from the truth. Intelligence can always be developed, even in adults. It only requires that people challenge themselves, explore unfamiliar topics and try to assimilate them into their understanding of the world.

You may be wondering why intelligence matters in a conversation. Quite simply, it is easier for intelligent people to connect the dots and expand on any topic that is presented to them. They are sources of interesting information and people tend to like someone they can learn from, as long as the person isn't condescending or hijacking the conversation.

To enhance your intelligence, make sure to:

1. **Expand your mind in a way that you enjoy**

People tend to shy away from this suggestion because they think it means they need to read a heap of books. While reading can definitely expand your mind, there are a variety of other options to better suit your preferences. You can learn about new topics by watching documentaries, educational YouTube videos, television shows, enrolling in a class, taking an online course, or perhaps by asking someone who knows more than you on a certain topic. Information can be transferred in countless ways. You just need to discover what way works best for you.

2. **Discuss a topic with someone who has a different opinion from you**

Learning to have a civil discussion with someone you disagree with is a highly valuable skill. By challenging our perspectives, they force us to reason and think critically, and let's face it, debates can be exciting. Even if you feel strongly that the other person could not be more wrong, it's an excellent exercise for developing your sense of logic. And sometimes we don't realize there's a flaw in our reasoning until we are faced with a challenger. We can learn from their good points as well as their flawed arguments. All we advise is that you keep it civil! Remember, attack the arguments, and not the person making them.

3. Practice explaining the new things you've learned

It's no use reading lots of information if we can't actually retain it. One way to ensure you keep all that new data in your head is to try and explain it to someone else. This can be anyone – a partner, a friend, or if you're feeling confident, a new acquaintance.

- **Humor**

To truly enjoy someone's company, there must be some level of humor. It forces us to take it easy, keep it light-hearted, and to see the joy in even the most absurd situations. Without humor, the world would be a miserable place, and this is why it's a vital component of the trifecta. Making someone laugh is an easy way to start developing a connection. In fact, humor is so powerful, it can make people overlook a range of negative qualities.

It's also important to note that having a good sense of humor also requires you to be able to take a joke. If someone pokes fun at you and they don't intend to be mean, try to see the humor in it! Laugh it off and don't be easily offended. And remember, the best kind of humor is not mean or degrading towards another person. Keep it smart and inoffensive.

1. Immerse yourself in comedic entertainment

There's no better way to understand the workings of good comedy than by finding comedic entertainment that you enjoy. Watch a funny TV show, movie, stand-up performance, or even YouTube videos. Expose yourself to a variety of comedy styles and choose the one you most enjoy. Try to stay away from comedy that revolves around pranks and slapstick humor. While it's totally fine to enjoy these, one shouldn't expect to learn anything from them.

2. **Practice seeing the absurdity in everyday scenarios**

This skill can be valuable not just for conversation skills but for life in general. It will teach you how to laugh in the face of disasters, and instantly ignite more positivity even on bad days. Laughter is, after all, one of the best remedies for all troubles. Life is filled with absurdity and ridiculousness, you just have to recognize it. The next time you find yourself annoyed by something, try turning it on its head and seeing it as a comedic scenario.

3. **Surround yourself with funny people**

We all know someone with a killer sense of humor, someone who's a joy to be around, and makes us laugh at the drop of a hat. A great way to become funnier or develop a better sense of humor is to spend time with funny people. Listen and laugh at their jokes, try to respond in a similarly lighthearted fashion, and try to learn from the way their humorize certain situations. Notice what they joke about, how they joke about it, and what exactly makes it funny. If there are jokes that fall a little flat, examine why. The best part of this humor-building tactic? You'll enjoy it immensely and spend more time with a friend!

- **Empathy**

Quite simply, empathy is the ability to put yourself in someone else's shoes. It means you can pick up on their emotions, and feel what they're feeling. It's more than just sympathy, empathetic individuals can feel other people's experiences as if they endured them as well.

Most of us are reasonably capable of cognitive empathy, which is when we understand emotion on an intellectual level, but we can't actually relate to what someone is feeling. Sometimes, we may not even really care, but we know what we're supposed to say to be polite. We can recognize that someone is sad, and we know how to act sympathetic, but there's no part of us that feels this person's sadness. We can think about emotions rationally, but all the while, we remain somewhat detached.

Cognitive empathy can prove useful in the workplace and quick everyday conversations, but if you're interested in deep connections, it won't be enough. Thankfully, developing your emotional empathy will also enhance your cognitive empathy, so why not start there?

1. **Become aware of your own emotions and engage in self-love**

It's an uncomfortable truth, but a truth nonetheless; it all begins with you and the way you deal with your emotions. If you're constantly suppressing your feelings and you never deal with them in an honest, healthy way, then it's likely you're unable to relate to the feelings of others. You may find that a part of you resists emotional empathy because it opens a locked box of feelings that you haven't yet dealt with.

2. **Learn the life story of someone you disagree with**

It's easy to empathize with a homeless person or a victim of abuse, but this doesn't prove you're an empathic person – only that you're not a sociopath. To truly build empathy, challenge yourself by delving deeper into the life of someone you disagree with. Try to detach yourself from the opposing view or opinion they hold, and instead try to see them as a unique human being who has led a complex life, no different to you or anyone you're friends with. The goal is not to like them or change your opinion, but instead, to see beyond your perspective and feel someone's experience. It's possible to empathize with someone's problems or issues, and not agree with the choices they made.

This exercise is likely to be more meaningful if it involves someone you know, but if you're not ready for such an encounter, it's possible to use a public figure you don't know personally. This step can be completed in a variety of ways. You can watch the biopic of a historical or famous figure, or if it's someone you know, you can try to get to know them over digital messages or in person. Build the conversation gradually so you don't come across as nosey. Start by asking them about their background or family and lead to questions about their goals or influences. You'd be surprised how much you can relate to someone you don't even like!

3. **Take the time to imagine what being someone else is like**

We've all done this for at least a fleeting second, but rarely do we take the time to do it in depth. Try it. It's an exercise you can do absolutely anywhere, and in any physical position. Choose someone you know reasonably well. Imagine what it was like to have their childhood. Consider what it was like to see their parents every single day. Think of what childhood needs might not have been met. What are this person's insecurities? Imagine what it's like to wake up every morning with those insecurities, and how it plays out in everyday interactions. What kind of situations would bring up those insecurities? Imagine what hardships could have led to those insecurities.

Visualize the experiences this person might have had to result in who they are today. And more than this, consider the privileges you have that this person doesn't. Even if they are wealthier and more successful than you, chances are there are still privileges you have that they don't. Perhaps you have a happier family, perhaps you've never been as unlucky in love, or maybe you have more supportive friends. Imagine what it's like to no longer have those privileges and acknowledge how different your life would be without them.

Three Steps to Becoming a More Interesting Person

Let's tackle a big question, shall we? Whether we admit it or not, we all want to become a more interesting person. But what does that really mean? Charisma is a major component, but that's not all there is to it. The trifecta of charm can also be considered a dominant influence over how interesting we are, but still, there's a little more to it than that. At the end of the day, being interesting comes with its own attitude – an attitude of openness and eclecticism.

Just think about all the experiences you've had with captivatingly interesting people. It's true that sometimes what's interesting can be subjective, but there are definitely some overarching traits. There tends to be the feeling that the other person is almost a treasure chest of stories and ideas. They have surprises up their sleeve. They know and have seen far more than you. They can't be caught or grasped, cause they are always one step ahead.

Let's use these experiences as a baseline, and figure out how we can emulate them.

1. Do interesting things

Doesn't that seem obvious? If you sit at home, watch TV, and stay in your comfortable bubble, you're not going to be very interesting to other people. We all use our experiences as a reference; if you haven't had many varied experiences, you're not going to have all that much to offer to conversations, unless it's with other people who also haven't seen that much. Accumulate fantastic, adventurous, and diverse experiences. Delve into the unknown and push the boundaries of your comfort zone. Do something you never thought you would do and expand your horizons. Collect interesting experiences and you'll become more interesting, in turn.

2. Think outside of the box

People are too focused on what they should be doing or saying that they miss the entire point of being interesting. Try thinking outside of the box or turning a situation on its head. This is different to behaving like a rebel or violating social codes; this just means responding in a way that is unusual. For example, if everyone is telling stories about how well-behaved their kid is, make things interesting by telling a story about the funniest thing your kid ever did, even if it was a little bit naughty. If all your friends are wearing modern bikinis, wear a classy high-waisted bikini styled from the 80s. If all your friends are discussing their biggest success at work, instead talk about the biggest failure that you learned the most from. Make situations more interesting by responding differently.

3. Be open-minded

No one likes a closed-minded person; the only ones who do are other closed-minded people who are closed-minded about the same things. Stop being so easily offended or shocked and replace those feelings with awe and curiosity. Not only will that make you more absorbent to interesting information, but it will also make you a more interesting conversationalist. The reason we like open-minded people is because they convey a sense of freedom. We actually don't experience closed-minded people as more moral, intelligent, or wise; they come across as caged by their own beliefs. Open-minded individuals can still have strong beliefs, but they are so comfortable and free that they can still listen to alternative opinions. We admire this sense of openness and freedom in others. Instinctively we feel that if a person embodies this attitude, they must have seen a lot and have a lot to share.

Developing all the qualities in this chapter will enhance your conversation skills tenfold. In reality, having better conversations begins with our frame of mind, our social abilities, and the experiences we've had. Work on developing all these skills, and you'll notice conversations coming alive in your presence.

Chapter 5 - Knowing Your Audience

You may be likable and charming, but no conversation arsenal is complete without the ability to read a room. A conversationalist that can read a room is able to pick up the thoughts, feelings and general personality of every person they observe or engage with. As we mentioned earlier, this skill is paramount to good communication as we need to understand the factors that influence whether our social tactics will succeed or not. The strategies to win over a shy person will likely annoy someone who is very outgoing, and vice versa. Someone who is in a bad mood will not be as receptive to certain social cues as someone who is in a great mood.

Microexpressions

We think that facial expressions tell us everything but that's not the whole truth. A smile doesn't always indicate happiness, and a serious expression doesn't necessarily indicate nervousness or displeasure. If you want to know how someone is truly feeling, pay attention to their microexpressions.

Microexpressions are nonverbal signals that last anywhere from a fraction of a second to a few seconds – but rarely longer than that. They may be recurring, but if they are permanent, then it's likely the person in question is not trying to hide their feelings at all. Microexpressions occur when we momentarily let our guard down and display our true reaction. Most people have been taught to act polite and always keep a tight rein on their true feelings, and this is why microexpressions are so fleeting. As soon as we feel ourselves slipping, we immediately return to the face we put on for the world.

The emotions we hide are not always negative. We may try to hide our euphoria while we're on a date with a person we really like, or we may try to hide our excitement if we're holding back good news before an official announcement.

Let's consider Rhonda again. While attending a friend's party, she meets a variety of different people with whom she interacts. Since she's not the most socially skilled person, she is met with a range of different reactions.

1. **Stress and impatience**

When Rhonda arrives at the party, she immediately comes across somebody she knows. She stops to talk to her old friend, and unbeknownst to her, she has stopped by a doorway, blocking someone from entering. The stranger stands behind her, clearing his throat, but Rhonda doesn't notice. He purses his lips and his nostrils flare for a moment. When Rhonda eventually takes notice, his jaw tightens before he regains his composure and walks to his intended destination.

2. **Frustration or anger**

While at the party, Rhonda runs into her ex. The relationship ended badly and mostly due to Rhonda's bad behavior. She doesn't recognize him immediately since he cut his hair and started wearing contact lenses. Sitting at a table with some acquaintances, she doesn't realize he is present as well, so she ignores him. The ex is fuming, still bitter about the way she treated him and even more now since she can't recognize him. While he fumes, he presses his lips together and continues to purse them intermittently.

3. **Disdain or dislike**

Rhonda notices two women having a conversation and she joins in. Unfortunately, she changes the topic and begins talking about herself quite incessantly. While Rhonda talks, one woman looks at her askance, only making eye contact with the corner of her eye. She keeps her head tilted away from Rhonda, a sign that she is not enthusiastic about this newcomer's presence and may even feel superior to her. She resists the urge to roll her eyes and in doing so her eyelids flutter with more blinks than usual, sending the message, "The nerve of this woman!"

4. Disagreement and contempt

Later on, Rhonda converses with a teacher and makes the argument, "Schools are killing the creativity of children." The teacher disagrees strongly with this, though he still tries to act polite. For a moment, he furrows his brows and asks, "How so?" When furrowed brows accompany narrowed eyes, it indicates disagreement or skepticism, but if the eyes are wide, this signals curiosity. As Rhonda continues, the teacher begins to feel a little contemptuous. One side of his mouth curls up very briefly while the other side remains still. Many people misinterpret this expression as a 'half-smile,' but this is incorrect. This is a classic sign of contempt, especially if the mouth is tight.

5. Fear

Someone who had a bad experience with Rhonda at a different party sees her approaching. As she notices Rhonda, her eyes widen for a brief moment, conveying a sense of vigilance. Fear is most easily identified by looking at the eyes. The mouth also reacts by widening horizontally. This is different from a smile where the corners are upturned, when fear is introduced, the corners pull back horizontally towards the ears.

6. Excitement or happiness

Even though Rhonda had negative impressions on a lot of people, the person who invited her to the party is happy to see her. Rhonda's friend is in the middle of a serious discussion with someone else, so she's trying to not look too happy, but when she notices Rhonda, her eyes look a bit brighter. Even though she's not smiling, both corners of her mouth turn up very slightly.

The Six Types of Communicators & How to Win Them Over

Social psychologists have discovered there are six major communication styles. While each of us is more likely to communicate in one of these styles naturally, we can actually learn how to use the talents and traits of all the other styles. For the most part, each type of communicator responds best to those who communicate in the same way, but not all the time. See if you can determine which type you are. And most importantly, figure out how you would approach the other different styles.

- **Noble**

Straightforward, focused, tells it like it is

These communicators tend to make great leaders as they have no qualms about saying what needs to be said and participating in the difficult conversations. They are practical, direct, and many people respond well to them since they are always honest. They are not concerned with the feelings of others, preferring to be upfront and straightforward. This doesn't mean they are unfeeling people, they simply don't factor in emotions when they are speaking. Though they usually don't have bad intentions, sensitive people can become upset at what they say since it's often not worded in a considerate manner. They are uncomplicated and usually quite predictable.

To win a Noble communicator over, you must be clear, direct, and confident. Avoid overly flowery language as they don't see the point and will see it as frivolous fluff. Focus on the 'what' and 'how,' since Nobles are most concerned with the practical details than anything else. Give them all the information upfront as they won't chase you for extra details. Other than these general rules, you'll find you can say almost anything to a Noble since they are only concerned with truth and reality.

- **Socratic**

Expressive, persuasive, intellectual, detailed

Unlike Noble communicators, Socratic individuals enjoy the long, drawn out discussions with lots of details. These communicators tend to clash with Nobles since their methods of communication are almost completely opposite. It is rare that a Socratic communicator gets into a short chat; as soon as they open their mouth, it's easy for them to get lost in a tangent or a long, flowery anecdote. When they tell stories they add a lot of background information, preferring to present the whole picture. At times, they can seem to be lecturing.

To befriend a Socratic, listen to their long-winded stories with your full attention, and better yet, ask them questions. They enjoy interesting and unique individuals, so make sure to tickle their intellect. Bring up unusual but fascinating topics, and join them as they delve deeply into them with their hundreds of questions and insightful analyses. They prefer to deal with ideas, instead of feelings, though they are more receptive to emotions than Nobles.

- **Reflective**

Patient, understanding, sensitive, wants to bond

If you're a reflective communicator, there are likely a lot of people in your life who run to you with their problems. For better or for worse, people enjoy seeking out support from reflectives since they are known for being understanding and having great listening skills. Reflectives like to connect on an emotional basis and usually aren't that interested in sharing strong opinions. It doesn't come naturally to a reflective communicator to be assertive or direct, so they can be dishonest or even deceptive. They would prefer to not see anyone's feelings hurt, so they say what needs to be said to keep conversation harmonious. Reflectives are the most likely communicators to get interrupted or overlooked in conversation, since they usually don't express themselves in a strong or confident manner.

To win a Reflective over, open up a little and show some vulnerability. Find common ground with them and share your mutual passions or interests. To really capture a Reflective's attention, ask them questions and encourage them to open up to you as well. They are so used to listening to other people and letting someone else take the spotlight that they can feel overlooked. Give them some kind attention and you'll win them over, for sure.

- **Candidate**

Pleasant, talkative, analytical, wants to be liked

When we combine the Socratic and Reflective styles, we get the Candidate communicator. Candidates are warm, chatty, and usually have a pleasant air about them. They enjoy connecting with others by telling stories, and will always make the effort to keep conversation harmonious. When a problem arises, they believe that talking is the best solution, and they do so in an emotionally engaged manner. They are more truthful than someone with only a Reflective style, but they still try their best to avoid messy conflict.

To get on their good side, turn on your good listening skills and be patient while they talk. If you stop paying attention or end a conversation abruptly, the Candidate will likely feel very annoyed. Since they also have Reflective attributes, they are a lot more receptive to other points of view than a Socratic communicator alone. Win them over by really engaging with them, sharing genuine parts of yourself, and listening closely to their long, sometimes emotional, stories.

- **Magistrate**

Intense, argumentative, persuasive

The Noble and Socratic styles fuse together to create the big presence of the Magistrate. These individuals can be incredibly eloquent and persuasive, but while they excel as public speakers, they can be a little slow in their interpersonal relationships. It takes them longer to grasp individual needs and sensitivities, so they can sometimes act out of line and offend people closest to them. When we witness a Magistrate communicator speaking, it can seem like they'd make a phenomenal leader. Oftentimes, it can come across like a monologue or a grand speech. Unfortunately, Magistrates tend to divide audiences and at their worst, can be preachy and overbearing. You either love them or you hate them. In their personal lives, they can be argumentative, and they may even get into trouble at work.

To get close to a Magistrate, be unafraid of serious, deep discussions. They don't shy away from the dark topics that, they feel, convey the real truth of life. It's also necessary that you understand how to speak calmly and rationally in heated discussions without flying off the handle. Otherwise you may find yourself in a full-blown argument with a Magistrate. Also make sure to listen closely to the Magistrate as they feel strongly that what they're saying needs to be heard. To flatter them, make them feel like the revolutionary they think they are.

- **Senator**

Strategic, adaptable, observant, versatile

The most complex of the six, the Senator is often considered the most clever communication style. In conversation, the way they speak and the things they say are all carefully calculated to produce the outcome they desire. They have the unique ability to combine the skills of the other five styles to create a predetermined effect. They may speak like a Noble, but also have the listening skills of a Reflective. They are highly unpredictable, and many people who try to get to know them may perceive them as fickle.

Trying to coax a Senator into your corner is no easy task. Of the six communicators, they are definitely the most difficult to catch. This is because they are always changing, and often their behavior is determined by what they hope to achieve. This is not always a selfish pursuit, sometimes the goal can be to help other people get along. The exact goal depends on the individual personality. We advise observing Senators closely and paying attention to the transitions between communication styles. One can often identify what their goal is by noticing what method of communication they are using at that moment. Reflect whichever style they appear to be using.

Conversation Tips for Special Audiences

As we've demonstrated, conversation tactics are not the same for everyone. And even though we've covered a wide range of personality types already, there are a few others we still haven't accounted for.

Children

It shouldn't be so scary to talk to tiny humans, but many people don't have experience with children. If you have to meet a new partner's kid or bond with a younger cousin, it will not serve you well to be filled with anxiety – though it wouldn't be completely unfounded. After all, children can't talk about the same topics as adults. And what if you accidentally say something that scares them?

The reality is, it's not as difficult as you think, and children are a lot smarter than people give them credit for. Children tend to respond positively when adults lower themselves to their height. When you're not a looming giant, you're more approachable. When you speak, make sure to use positive language. Instead of just saying, "Your mom has told me a lot about you" try sweetening it up by saying "Your mom has told me so much about how talented and smart you are!" Remember that kids love the idea of adventure, so if you're going to tell them any stories, make sure it has a hint of adventure. And ask them questions about what they enjoy. Kids will warm up to you when they can talk about whatever excites them.

When you talk to a kid, fully embrace silliness and you'll definitely get on their good side. And remember, do not ever correct a child when they are speaking playfully! If they said they visited the land of unicorns, do not say "Unicorns don't exist." Instead, ask them what it's like there and if they made any unicorn friends.

The Elderly

It's no secret that as people get older, they become less physically and mentally capable of behaving as they used to. One common mistake people make, however, is talking to them like they're children. While they may be a little slower, you'll find that most elderly individuals are still incredibly sharp, especially when you ask them about the passions of their life. Shoot them a few questions about how they met their life partner, the career they had, or where they came from, and you'll find that they suddenly regain all their wits (provided none of these questions trigger something traumatic!) and enjoy sharing the fascinating stories they hold. Bear with them if their memory slows down, and allow them to find their thoughts.

Always speak to the elderly like the adults they are. Dumbing down your speech is not only rude, but it can actually do harm to their mental processes. Why? For the same reason you'd suffer if someone dumbed down their speech towards *you*. It lowers their self-esteem and quickens the decline of their cognitive abilities because no one is allowing them to use their mind properly.

There are as many communication styles as there are human beings in the world. No two people communicate in the exact same way – but this guide will help you navigate the major personalities. To identify what their exact style is like, consider their age, background, culture, interests, and their general nature. Everything is a clue; pay attention.

Chapter 6 - Building Deep Connections

At the end of the day, we all crave something beyond lighthearted banter or party discussions. We want to bond with others. We want to see our humanity mirrored in another person, and we want to mirror theirs. Many will even argue that this is what life is all about – learning to live in harmony with others so we can help each other excel. Whatever you believe, it stands true for everyone: we all need deep connections. Without them, we can even become more susceptible to mental illness.

Since we all need it to thrive, you'd think it would be easy to make lasting and deep connections. But for the majority of us, they are few and far between. Often the most meaningful connections we have are with people we've known for a long time.

There are many reasons we may find this feat difficult. Sometimes it's because we're afraid of intimacy. Sometimes it's because we can be judgmental, and we want to believe there's nothing we could possibly have in common with the people around us. And of course many times, we just don't have the necessary social skills. We want a meaningful connection, but we just don't know how to get from A to B.

Here's some good news: it's actually not as difficult as you think.

Conversation Tricks to Instantly Build Rapport with Someone

1. **Try to reflect their speaking style**

Pay attention to the rhythm, length, and word choices with which someone speaks. To build rapport, try and mirror their style of speech. If there are words they use often, work them into your side of the dialogue as well. It's important, when doing this, to not copy them entirely, or they'll feel like you're making fun of them. To avoid this, a good rule of thumb is to never mimic someone's accent.

2. Seek out their advice

Instead of asking for someone's opinion, ask for their advice. Doing this will strengthen your bond. Why? For starters, you come across as being genuine (only honest people can admit they need advice!) and second of all, you're showing them you think they're a credible source of feedback. After this interaction, they are also likely to feel invested in the issue they advised you on and they may want to keep up with what happens. Just make sure you pay close attention to them and listen to what they're saying carefully.

3. Combine ideas

You don't have to be at a work meetup to brainstorm; you can do this with anyone. All it involves is playing off their ideas and expanding on them. When you brainstorm with someone, whether casually or seriously, you show them you've been paying close attention to them and that you take their ideas seriously. In addition to this, you may satisfy their need for expansion, by showing that you have something to offer them intellectually.

4. Paraphrasing

When we paraphrase what someone says, we repeat what they said in our own words. The paraphrase should always be combined with another statement such as "I understand." Or, it can be turned into a question with the addition of something to the effect of "Is that right?" Paraphrasing shows that you've listened, understood, and empathized with what they've said. For example, if your friend says, "I'm an insomniac so please excuse me if I seem a little out of it," you could say, "I understand. You didn't get enough sleep, so of course you feel exhausted and disoriented." By saying this, you're not adding any new information, only rephrasing the previous statement slightly.

5. Ask questions that involve 'how' and 'why'

If you're not sure what kind of questions to ask, think of something that begins with 'how' or 'why.' These types of questions create bonds because you're asking your conversation partner to search themselves for more elaborate and meaningful answers. For example, if your friend is talking about a high-pressure meeting she just finished. You could ask "How do you feel about it now?" or "Why do you think it went so well?"

Building rapport is essential to creating a bond with empathy and connection, but we won't get there immediately. It involves a lot more than conversation tactics.

How to Form Meaningful Relationships

1. Let people in

All the other points on this list mean nothing if you don't let people in. Don't act cold and aloof as this forms a barrier between yourself and others. Instead, try to exude an inviting aura and allow them to get to know you, as much as you get to know them. People often make the mistake of feeling like a victim when other people don't take an interest in getting to know them. Do not fall into this victim complex. Instead, ask yourself: am I showing this person that I can be trusted? Am I allowing people to get close to me? Am I showing them what makes me a good friend?

2. Balance giving and taking

If your friend bought you lunch at your last hang-out, buy them a drink or meal at your next hang-out. Return generosity with generosity. If you aren't in a good place financially, offer to do something else for them. There is beauty in having a friend or family member that would do anything for us, but our responsibility as a good person is to never ask them to do *everything* for us. If you come to the realization that you've been talking about your problems non-stop for the last hour, take the time to ask your close connection how they are, and make sure to offer them the same patience. Always be aware of when you might be asking for too much. And if you must, then ensure you make it up to them.

It's also important to note that the reverse should also be avoided. If your friend continuously asks you for a lot, be honest about how you feel and create some boundaries.

3. Make time to maintain the bond

Once we form a bond with a new friend or partner, we need to make the effort to nurture this relationship. It doesn't matter how well we get along with someone else – if we never make time for them in our lives, this bond will slowly dissipate. And when a reconnection is made in the distant future, it'll feel like you're starting all over again.

The act of making time is a powerful one, and it sends an important message: I care enough about you to always find time for you. If one party embarks on a long travel experience, or moves to a different city, make the effort to do a weekly or fortnightly catch-up session on the phone. Avoid having a dynamic where you only speak when one person needs a shoulder to cry on. Even partners that live together must find time in their busy schedules to maintain the bond. Creating quality time is a necessary part of keeping a connection alive.

4. Eradicate all competitive behavior

When we're close to someone, it's easy to start comparing ourselves to them. If your friend or partner is further along in their career than you are, never allow feelings of envy to drive your actions. It's perfectly normal for a jealous thought to cross your brain, but never let it trigger a decision that affects them. It's totally fine to think, "Gee, Adam is really having an affect on all the girls at this party. I wish I could do that." But it is not okay to start telling someone about his most embarrassing moment just to take him down a peg. Recognize that you both have different strengths and weaknesses, and that life is not a competition. Look for inspiration in your relationships, not competition.

5. Know the purpose your relationship serves

Each person in our life helps us in a slightly different way. Recognizing the greater purpose they serve can ignite feelings of appreciation and will ultimately help us strengthen the bond. The gifts they bring to our lives are far more specific than just giving us emotional support or preventing us from feeling bored. If you think about it, each person we know provides us with a unique lesson. See if you can identify the people who continuously teach you these lessons – and work out which ones you teach other people.

- Embrace everything that makes you different.
- It's okay to cry and talk about your feelings.
- Opposites attract and help each other grow.
- Everything can be fun if you let it be.
- The world is full of amazing experiences and you need to chase them all.
- We must always face ourselves exactly as we are and strive to be better.
- Just enjoy things as they are, there's no need to make it complicated.
- A true friend is with you during your darkest hours.

The Habits of Emotionally Intelligent People

Remember when we discussed how magnetic individuals are adept at emotional self-sufficiency? That's a major attribute of emotional intelligence. An emotionally intelligent individual can not only sense, understand, and empathize with the feelings of others, they also have a firm grasp on their own emotions.

Believe it or not, emotional intelligence is a bigger indicator of one's success than their IQ. While an IQ is more likely to earn you a particular job, your level of emotional intelligence will determine whether you keep that job, or whether you get promoted. More than this, however, emotional intelligence is vital for fulfilling personal relationships, whether it's with family, friends, or romantic partners. Some people are born with an intrinsic gift for emotional intelligence, but it's completely possible for others to learn and develop the skill over time. Let's examine the life-altering habits of emotionally intelligent people.

- **They always find common ground**

When in conversation with someone, emotionally intelligent people focus on the similarities instead of the potential conflicts. It doesn't matter who it is or how different that person seems to be, they always converse with the intention of finding common interests and values. Even if the person they're talking to openly disagrees with them about something, individuals with a high EQ choose to focus on the similarities. When faced with conflict, they have the maturity to say, "Let's agree to disagree."

- **They are self-aware**

Self-awareness is a key attribute of emotional intelligence. This means that an individual has a good understanding of who they are, how they feel, what their triggers are, and how they are most likely to react in a given scenario.

Let's take Sally, for instance. She's has an extremely high EQ. After a bad day at work, she recognizes that she's feeling anxious and sad. Her friends invite her to have dinner at the mall. She knows that when she's sad, she is more likely to shop and overspend, so she has the self-awareness to realize that being near a shopping mall is not a good idea.

- **They are masters of self-discipline and self-management**

Remember when Sally recognized that going to the mall on a bad day would have a terrible outcome? Awareness is one thing, but having the discipline to say no is another. Self-awareness and self-discipline go together like bread and butter. After all, what's the point of being aware of the best course of action if you can't bring yourself to actually take that action?

Emotionally intelligent people are not slaves to their impulses. They are not prone to big bursts of anger or indignation; they deal with their feelings privately and if something must be done, they go about it maturely. They have the strength of mind to suppress behavior that will only cause damage and destruction, even if it causes momentary agitation. They don't expect other people to take care of their feelings, instead they take care of themselves.

- **They are always aware of subtext**

Everyone knows there's a big difference between the words people speak and what they're *actually* saying. High EQ individuals are always aware of this subtext. They are masters at interpreting tones of voice, word pacing, and the general vibe given off by each person they meet. With everything that they gage through observation, they are able to understand what's not being said. Intuition and 'gut feelings' can also help with deciphering subtext. If you get a strong feeling about something, chances are you're onto some subtext.

- **They steer clear from blame games**

Emotionally intelligent people are masters of accountability and acceptance. When something goes wrong, they resist the urge to point the finger elsewhere. They recognize that it usually takes more than one person to create a certain situation. If we find out a friend talked about us behind our back, it's easy to put all the blame on them and say they shouldn't have been doing that. But what if your friend was saying she's angry because you owe her a lot of money and she doesn't think you'll ever pay her back? It's important that we recognize our part in every situation. It's not about feeling guilty, it's about admitting that we have more power than we realize and owning up to the repercussions.

It's true that sometimes we can fault one person for something that goes wrong. If you took all safety precautions and someone robbed you anyway, it seems very clear who should be blamed. Not you, but them. Avoiding the blame game doesn't mean you can never say that someone else made a mistake; it means that you don't get stuck in a loop of blame where you cause yourself to suffer more than you need to. It's the difference between thinking "That man made a mistake" and "What an awful man. How dare he? Now everything is ruined and it's all because of him."

Why Self-Compassion is Important for Healthy Relationships

A well-known misconception about fulfilling relationships is the idea that we need to give, give, and give to our closest companions. Kindness and empathy towards others are important parts of every relationship, that's true, but it's imperative that we never neglect our own needs. In fact, a good rule of thumb is to treat yourself the way you would treat a good friend. We would never ask a friend to give until she has nothing, and so we should never ask that of ourselves.

Self-compassion helps us recharge so we can continue to do our best for the world we live in. When we drain ourselves of energy, we are more prone to depression, moodiness, or general exhaustion. We drain ourselves of everything we need to continue being a good friend. Indirectly, self-compassion helps the people we care about as well.

Here are the ways in which we can show ourselves self-compassion in our everyday relationships:

- Your friends want you to stay out late for a big night out, but you're exhausted from work and don't really want to go. Instead of forcing yourself to go out because everyone wants you to, put self-care first. Tell your friends: "I'm going to take a raincheck and stay home to rest. I'm extremely tired, so I know you understand. Let's do something else soon!"

- You're with a group of people who are all sharing raunchy sex stories. You've always been a more private person and you start to feel uncomfortable with the topic. When everyone looks at you expectantly, waiting for a story, don't feel pressured. Just say: "I'd prefer to keep this part of my life private, so I'm going to pass." Or if you're with a closer group of friends, feel free to tell them, "I'm not really comfortable sharing such intimate stories. Could we change the topic?"
- You run into a friend that you aren't very close to. She hears you broke up with your partner and is pressuring to tell you everything that happened, even though you don't want to talk about it. Be kind to yourself, and don't give in to pressure if it causes you distress. Tell her: "I'm not ready to talk about it yet. It's still hard to think about, so I'll have to tell you another time. Thanks for your concern."
- If a family member said something extremely hurtful and they suddenly want to see you, be compassionate towards yourself and ask yourself if you're ready or if you even want to. When someone hurts us it can take a while before we feel safe around them again. This is not our fault, and we should always make sure we are ready for future interactions.

Healthy and deep relationships require both parties to be taken care of. To develop more fulfilling connections, make sure both sides get what they need every time – and yes, that means you too! Make sure boundaries are respected and balance is always attained.

Chapter 7 - Difficult Situations & Social Blunders

It's bound to happen at some point. Unfortunately, it's usually when you least expect it. You think everything is going swimmingly and feel like you're as smooth as honey, but then the unexpected happens. Perhaps you say something you shouldn't have – an easy flub or a major no-no – or perhaps the circumstances are out of your control, and a real jerk comes out of nowhere, derailing all your well-played moves and making you look like a fool.

We're not perfect and neither is anyone else. Awkward moments *will* happen and some of them will be mind-numbingly cringeworthy. In addition to this, rude people are aplenty, and we're going to encounter them whether we like it or not. To become a master of conversation, it's necessary that you understand how to diffuse a difficult social situation. There may be rocky roads ahead, so it's best to gear up.

How to talk your way out of difficult or awkward situations

Don't just sit back and go red in the face. There are many ways we can use speech and conversation to mitigate a difficult conversation. You'd be surprised by how much we can accomplish with these quick tips.

- **You offended someone**

There are many reasons you could find yourself in this difficult position. You might have encountered someone who was easy to offend, or maybe, just maybe, you said something legitimately terrible. The first step is always to apologize, whether you mean it or not, and let them know you didn't mean to offend them. The second step is up to you.

i) Insist you chose your words wrongly and that it wasn't what you meant to say. If you can, amend what you said with better, less offensive phrasing. You can also chalk it down to a lack of sleep or fatigue, and tell them you're not as articulate as you normally are.

ii) Take the fall, be vulnerable and shift power from you to the other party. For example, let's say you accidentally insulted the way your friend dressed for a party and she is noticeably upset. Clear things up immediately by saying, "I'm sorry. Actually it's me, not you. I'm feeling very self-conscious in this outfit, and you look great. I'm a little jealous, so I projected how I feel about myself onto you."

- **Someone openly insults you**

Awful, shocking, humiliating; these are some of the words you could use to describe the moment when someone insults you. It may be direct and outright, or heavily implied. Either way, it will likely shake you to your core.

The first step is to consider whether we were truly insulted. Oftentimes, we can perceive brutally honest statements as insulting, but really they are just based on a harsh truth we don't want to accept. If we find the insult is more factual than not, then accept what's being said, apologize if necessary, and adjust your behavior, taking into account this new feedback.

You may also figure out the insult was real, and that a person really did just attack your character. In that case, you may follow any of these steps:

i) Use humor to undermine and ridicule the insult. This one takes some skill but when done correctly, you can win over an entire audience.

ii) Stand up for yourself in an honest and calm way. This does not mean fighting back. If someone calls you an idiot for not knowing something, you can respond by saying, "I'm not an idiot. No one knows everything and we're all learning here." By defending yourself in a mature manner, you'll bound to come out of the situation on-top.

iii) Let it slide but bring it up in private, afterwards. If you're not quick on your feet, it's okay to say nothing or laugh it off for the time being. Later on, you can take the person aside and confront them about what they said. This option is more likely to get a meaningful reaction from the person who insulted you. After the heat of the moment, people often regret their mistakes. Be honest about how uncalled for and hurtful it was to be insulted. This direct confrontation may make this person apologize.

- **Someone tries to argue with you**

When we get into a conversation, most people make the effort to keep it harmonious. For many reasons, however, you may encounter someone with an argumentative approach. This can be because they feel passionately against something you said, or it may be down to their personality. Assuming you have no interest in entering this argument, you can follow any of these steps:

i) Say "Let's agree to disagree." Completely disengage from the heated discussion. Cut it off before it gets worse.

ii) Listen to the other person's point of view. At the end of the day, the person just wants you to see their side. Allow them to fill you in, all the while saying that you see their point. Acknowledge that they have interesting points, but avoid mentioning your opinion. Turning on your listening skills is another effective way to avoid an argument.

- **Someone hits on you obnoxiously and can't take a hint**

Women experience this more often than men. You could be anywhere, on a bus or at a party, and someone may decide to make a move. Through body language and the nature of your speech, you get across that you're not interested, but the flirty individual does not budge.

i) Tell them to stop. Sometimes it can feel like this is the worst thing you can do, but it's usually the most effective method. The other person can't take a hint so sometimes there is no other way but to tell them outright. It doesn't have to be rude if you're trying to let this person off gently. You could say, "You're making me feel uncomfortable. I'm really not interested. I have been trying to let you know discreetly, but perhaps I'm not being clear enough."

ii) Mention that you have a partner. In conversation, let slip that you have a boyfriend or girlfriend, or a husband or wife. If you can gush about them, the more likely they'll leave you alone. You can even do this if you don't have a partner; just be prepared to answer questions, if they ask.

iii) Seek out the company of a third person. If you're at a social gathering, ask someone else to join you or excuse yourself to join a different conversation. Don't be afraid to quietly tell another person (ideally of the same gender as you) that you need some help getting rid of an obnoxious flirt. Most people will sympathize with you and try to help.

- **You need to break up with a boyfriend or fire an employee**

These are some of the most difficult conversations to start. And yet, mastering how to do it can make a genuine difference in the rejected person's life. A bad rejection or relationship end can either lower someone's self-esteem, or empower them to grow. To ensure it's the latter instead of the former. Follow these tips.

i) Make the time and do it in person. Even though the situation is extremely uncomfortable for you, no doubt, don't rush through the talk and make the meeting as personal as possible. It's harder for the other person than it is for you, so make sure to allow them all the closure they need. If they don't get closure, there's a higher chance they'll take it badly and find it difficult to move on.

ii) Tell them the issues honestly, but also mention their potential. We should always be fairly honest about what's not working out. If you're breaking up with your partner because you feel like you're not compatible, it's okay to tell them that. But make sure to also mention something that will not make them feel like a failure. Empower them to find another partner or employer. If you're parting with them because of an existing problem, give them constructive advice for how to grow. Also be prepared for the possibility they will give you feedback as well.

iii) End the conversation on a positive note. It may be a sad and awkward occasion, but there's no reason it has to end on that note. Wish them good luck in all their future endeavours. Tell them you're so sure they'll find a job or partner that's right for them, very soon!

Coping with Difficult Personalities

It doesn't matter how many social tactics you have up your sleeve; when a difficult person comes into play, sometimes they can be intent on ruining the mood or heating up a conversation. For a number of difficult people, it is just the way they are, but it's important to note that for the majority of people, it could just be a bad day or a rough period in their life. While this doesn't excuse their behavior, it should encourage us to empathize with them and resist the urge to be nasty.

Before we discuss the specific types of difficult personalities, here are three general rules to keep in mind:

- Consider what their real need is. What is it they really want that they don't know how to get in a healthy way? There can be general needs that are common to certain personality types, but often they can be specific to the individual.

- Stay calm and listen to what they're saying before you respond.

- Take the high road and continue to treat them with respect.

1. **The Egomaniac**

Egomaniacs have an inflated sense of self-importance and somehow conversation always seems to lead back to how great they are. They can be overt egomaniacs, talking shamelessly about their accomplishments, but sometimes it can be subtle. Many attempt to seem like a normal person, but you'll find they don't really care about what you're saying, and if they do, they may display some competitiveness. To spot an egomaniac, look out for someone with extreme confidence. They will likely carry a sense of entitlement which manifests in an attitude of "This is so unfair!" over something minor. Egomaniacs are usually alone, but if they're not, they are accompanied by other egomaniacs or a very submissive partner.

The real need: Most times, what can appear as egomania is actually a deep insecurity and weak emotional foundation. Deep down inside, they feel there is something lacking so they must overpower this gut instinct by shouting about how great they are. If they don't do this, they will have to face their true feelings about themselves, and they are so weak, they cannot handle this reality. What they really need is recognition – but not about their surface accomplishments. Instead they need assurance about their deeper qualities. They have so much insecurity about their real self, that they overcompensate and show-off with the other aspects of their life they can control, such as what car they drive, who they've slept with, or how much money they make.

Sometimes, however, the egomaniac you've met is a sociopath. They do not feel remorse or empathy, and they can be extremely smart. These people do not crave recognition, and their need is simply to dominate others.

Solution: An egomaniac cannot take criticism well and is not capable of accountability, so you'd be wasting your time trying to get an apology. The best way to deal with them is to not take what they say seriously and avoid giving them the flattery that they desire. In discussions, only deal in facts and never emotions. Remember, they do not care about your emotions, only their own.

2. The Bully

No one likes a bully and if you encounter one, it's likely you're not the only person trying to fight him off. The bully enjoys shaming, humiliating, or singling out the people around him. He gets a noticeable thrill from catching someone off guard or seeing them speechless after he belittles them. Most of the time, a bully only acts this way when he's in group settings. One-on-one, you may find him to be quite insecure and standoffish, but not always. Adult bullies can cause just as much damage as child bullies, but unfortunately, they aren't confronted on their behavior as much; adults do not like admitting that they are dealing with a bully.

The real need: Bullies usually come from home lives where they were overpowered or bullied themselves. Their behavior is rooted in a feeling of having no control or power; this is why they seek out scenarios where they can feel powerful. Even if it's not rooted in a traumatic home life, the need of all bullies is similar: to feel powerful and superior by stirring someone's emotions and making them feel inferior.

Solution: Bullies enjoy inciting a reaction in their target, so whatever you do, act calm and avoid being reactive. Remain cool in the face of their aggression and they'll soon realize they can't get what they want from you. Realize that they are behaving from an immature, childlike need, so you must treat it as such. Do not give them the pleasure of feeling like they hold sway over your emotions. If you know this bully well, call them out on their behavior and do not let them get away with it.

3. The Victim

Make no mistake, the victim may look like a harmless, pathetic individual, but they can do a lot of damage, even without their realizing it. Victims always feel persecuted, like they're constantly getting the short end of the stick. They may accuse others of treating them differently or behaving cruelly towards them, even if no such thing occurred. These people love to talk about their personal problems. They are prone to oversharing and can do so for extended periods of time. If you try to bring up your own problems, they will respond with an attitude that says, "My problem is much worse." If a Victim causes harm to another individual, they have a hard time holding themselves accountable. They believe they cannot hurt others, since they are the real ones hurting.

The real need: At some point in the Victim's life, they did not get the empathy or sympathy they needed from an important person, such as a parent. During some life event, they were truly the victim in the situation but no one recognized this. Because they didn't get the closure they needed, they continued to carry this need for sympathy into the other areas of their life. The Victims are in need of empathy, but more than anything, they also need boundaries. They need to realize what happened to them in the past is separate from what's happening now.

Solution: To sidestep all the drama of the Victim, do not play into their hands. Once you get them started on their troubles, it's hard for them to stop. Instead, deal with them positively and give them the opposite of what they want to hear. Say things like, "I'm sorry to hear that, but it's great that at least you had wonderful friends to help you!" Even if they are not convinced by your positivity, it will show them they cannot drag you down into their self-pitying hole. If you know the person well, give them boundaries. For example, say you'll listen to them complain for five to ten minutes, but after that, you are only interested in discussing solutions to the problems.

4. **The Negative Nancies**

Like Victims, negative individuals can come across as nice people. Once you get into a more in depth conversation, however, you'll notice one thing: they exude so much negativity! They are distrustful and always see the downside of every issue. They will discourage you from the slightest risk, and you may leave interactions with them feeling more worried, and a lot less excited.

The real need: In the negative person's eyes, they are not being negative, only realistic. By being negative, they are attempting to gain control over the situation by staying aware of the worst case scenario. At some point in the past, they let their guard down and something bad happened that was out of their control. Ever since then, they've needed to feel like they have control, so they always expect the worst case scenario. Unfortunately, by doing this, it tends to become a self-fulfilling prophecy.

Solution: Counter their negativity with positivity, but remember that it's not your responsibility to make them happy. Show the Negative Nancy that they do have control over creating a positive outcome. And show them that infusing negativity into every situation can actually bring about a negative outcome. Consider sharing some interesting stories from your life where you took a risk and it resulted in something highly positive.

5. The Contrarians

It's normal to have a dose of contrarianism in us, but true contrarians take it to an extreme. It doesn't matter what you say, even if it's completely reasonable, the contrarian will always take the opposing side. They love to debate and don't really care what people think about them. Oftentimes, they'll even play Devil's advocate, taking on an unpopular opinion, just to spark a good argument. Anyone who loves debating may get along with a contrarian, but even then, the constant challenge can get exhausting.

The real need: The needs of contrarians can vary. Sometimes the individual really wants to come across as a unique person – someone who stands out of the crowd. Other times it can come from a genuine distrust of authority; so whatever the leading opinion is, they immediately expect something suspicious behind it. When they stand up against a perceived authority, it is a rebellion and an attempt to feel superior. Sometimes they feel they are doing the right thing, but other times it is purely to satisfy their own ego. If they can own you in an argument, then in their mind, they have asserted their superiority over some authority force.

Solution: Contrarians are some of the most likely personalities to start arguments. The best way to avoid it is to focus on finding common ground with them. Since they are so passionate about certain issues, a "let's agree to disagree" approach may not always work. In this case, try to take a listening approach. Instead of arguing, question them about their opinions and get them to explain it to you further. It cannot become an argument if you don't insert your opinion into the matter.

If you do argue with a contrarian, stick to the facts. Do not get noticeably frustrated or overcome with emotion as some contrarians enjoy this. Another way to avoid a debate is to get the contrarian to tell you their opinion first. That way you'll know how to agree with them and prevent an argument.

When is it okay to lie?

We're all told that lying is bad, but it's not always that simple. We should never lie to manipulate or mislead, but there are many occasions where lying may be helpful or beneficial. If you're not sure whether it's okay to lie in a particular situation, ask yourself these questions. The more times you answer 'yes,' the more likely it is that you *shouldn't lie*.

- If I lie, will I prolong a situation that's harmful to someone?

- If I lie, am I enabling someone's unhealthy delusion?
- If I lie, will I save myself from potential danger?
- If I tell the truth, will I lower their self-esteem?
- If I tell the truth, will I hurt someone's feelings over something they have no control of?

Chapter 8 - Using Conversation to Get What You Want

The best conversationalists are constantly using words to wield their way. It can be something as minor as convincing a friend to come out with you or as major as convincing your boss you need a massive raise. And if you're not doing it, chances are it's been done to you. The craziest part is you're not going to even be aware of the most successful ploys against you. The most persuasive conversationalists can slip by unnoticed like a black cat in the dark.

As we've demonstrated, it's never just about what you say, it's also largely about how you behave. Your behavior will set the stage for your words, and will strongly influence how they come across. That's why, in the arena of persuasion, we must also begin with behavioral tactics.

Subtle ways of showing dominance

Showing real dominance is not just about being a jerk or acting cocky. In fact, if you're coming across as a nasty person, you're just displaying aggressive behavior. This takes no skill and it's not a sustainable method of taking or maintaining power. You're playing on everyone's need to defend themselves against violence by cornering them, and making them feel they have no other choice. True dominance, on the other hand, is achieved by getting others to follow your lead willingly.

If two people, equal in experience and skill, are interviewed for the same job, dominant behavior can make one party appear more competent. Why? It's about far more than what you see on paper. A person who displays dominant behavior shows potential leadership abilities and the big winner, confidence. It presents the illusion that their competence is stronger than the other person, even if it may not be true. Even outside of the professional arena, dominant behavior makes it more likely for people to listen to you and it increases your level of attractiveness to the opposite sex.

That said, you don't need to become a total alpha to succeed, you just need to keep some of these tips in mind for when the right scenario reveals itself.

1. Make your body bigger

The psychology behind this sign of dominance has its roots in our animalistic natures. In the animal kingdom, many beasts display the largeness of their size in order to intimidate the other contenders. The one that appears biggest wins by default, without the need to incite violence. Humans can also do this to successfully assert their dominance. To make your body look big, open out your chest, stand tall, and if it doesn't look unnatural, put your hands on your hips. In addition to the above, women can also show dominance by wearing high heeled shoes.

2. Walk through the middle of the room

When in a crowded room, people have a tendency to make their body smaller and move through whatever side of the room has the most space. Instead of adjusting to the room, try making the room adjust to you. Walk through the middle of the room, even if there's a crowd, and expect people to move out of the way for you. Most people want to avoid bumping into someone, so they'll budge if you refuse to.

3. Sit at the head of the table

The person who sits at the head of the table oversees everything. They can keep a watchful eye on anyone, and they occupy the only seat that does not share its level with someone else. The next time you're with a group, sit in that dominant seat.

4. Use hand gestures and touch

To assert dominance, make good use of your hands. Make sure to initiate handshakes by extending your hand first. Then remember, to shake firmly. While you're talking, use your hands expressively, but keep your wrists strong and never limp. Dominant individuals also touch other people, even if they don't know them very well. This is not sexual. This can be a friendly knock on the shoulder, a slap on the knee, or perhaps even a hand placed on their back followed by a directive statement like, "Let's get you another drink."

5. Speak with a louder voice

Studies have shown that the loudest voice in the group is seen as the most dominant. Even if they speak less than others, it will make all others pause due to its volume alone. Use your lungs and diaphragm to achieve a louder voice. As you attempt this, do not yell or shout while you're in conversation, as this will only alarm and possibly scare away the people around you.

It is also extremely important to ensure that your voice never gets higher in pitch when you converse. When we are in the presence of someone we feel is superior, our voices immediately get higher pitched than usual. Keep your voice at its normal pitch at all times to avoid coming across as submissive.

Now that we've got our behavior under control, let's get a back-and-forth going.

Persuasion Techniques for all Situations

1. Framing

When it comes to swaying people in a direction of your choice, the art of framing is a classic. When we frame something, we highlight whichever attributes will help our argument best, while paying less attention or even hiding its less appealing factors.

Let's say you're trying to convince a friend of yours to go on holiday with you and your family. To help your argument, you should mention the beautiful location, the fun activities, the luxurious hotel rooms, the attractive locals, etc. And you should avoid talking at length about your annoying Aunt Margaret and the fact that it'll be crowded during the tourist season. If your friend already suspects the risks, then acknowledge them, but emphasize the aspects that will help your argument.

2. The yes ladder

This psychological technique has proven successful at eliciting a 'yes' response when used correctly. The first step is to think of the big question you need a positive response to. Once you've determined what this is, start thinking of smaller, relevant asks that are more likely to get a 'yes' response. Gradually work your way through the easy asks, before ending with the big question.

For example, let's say you're trying to convince your family to go on holiday, but you know they're hesitant to leave their normal routine. You would start off with questions like, "Do you ever feel like there's so much in the world you haven't seen yet?" and "Do you agree that life is most fulfilling when you're taking risks and experiencing something new?" You could even throw in, "Do you ever feel like you're wasting your life playing it too safe?" Chances are they will say yes to all these questions. Once you've extracted all the 'yes' answers, your big ask has a much higher chance of success. Finally, you ask, "Perhaps it's time, then, to go on holiday and finally have some new experiences?"

3. The unreasonable request

If the yes ladder isn't quite your approach, then why not try the opposite? Instead of building yourself up to a big ask, start with an unreasonable ask. It's important to make sure, however, that you don't actually want this unreasonable ask. You're expecting the other person to say no to this so that when you finally get to your smaller request, it seems a lot more reasonable. For example, let's say you're asking someone to donate to your charity. Start off by saying, "Would you be interested in making a $200 donation?" When they shake their head and say no, you can finally say, "We understand. In that case, how about just a $10 donation?"

4. Emphasize the benefits

To effectively convince someone of a course of action, you must consider the benefits they'll experience. Never assume that people will do anything simply out of the kindness of their hearts, especially if you're not a close friend or relative. When you're trying to persuade someone, really emphasize the benefits they'll receive if they agree to what you're saying. This works across the board, for all situations. If there's a reason they're reluctant, show them how one of the benefits will help them solve that problem. If you're trying to convince a coworker to get lunch with you, but he's too busy making last minute touches on a project, don't just emphasize how great the food will be. Be specific to his benefits. For example, you could say that he'll probably work much more efficiently once he eats some good food.

5. Speed up or slow down your speech

A known persuasion rule is that if an audience is most likely to disagree with what you're saying, increase the rate at which you're speaking. We see this a lot in salesmen where they will talk faster so that the person they're speaking to becomes overwhelmed with information. This gives them less time to notice things that may be incorrect and they are less likely to form a counter-argument.

If you think the odds are in your favor, the opposite will be beneficial. Slow down your speech if you think there's a strong possibility that your audience will agree with you. This will ensure that others feel more satisfied about their decision. If you give them time to assess all the information you've presented, they will feel as though they came to the conclusion completely on their own. They won't feel as though they were subjected to persuasion tactics, and this will make them happier with their decision.

Three Tricks to Seduce Someone through Conversation

First of all, let's get one thing straight. If someone has zero attraction towards you, this section can't turn those tables. In fact, you'll be hard pressed to find anything that can. It can, however, turn a little bit of attraction into a lot of attraction. If there's something there, it can be kicked up a notch with these tips.

1. Fractionation

Fractionation is a Neuro-Linguistic Programming tool and its original intentions were not for seduction. In fact, it was used to enhance a patient's state of hypnosis during hypnotherapy. Today, it is thought to be a controversial technique for seduction, but one thing is for sure: it works. It involves using a hot-then-cold dynamic where desire is elevated through intermittent reinforcement.

It is easy to use this seduction method in an unethical way, but we don't advise resorting to abusive behavior. Instead, consider the many ethical ways we can use fractionation to stir desire.

- Incorporate hot-then-cold conversation topics. During ordinary conversation, we tend to start with light-hearted conversation. And if we care to prolong the interaction, it often deepens until it is at its most intense state, and both parties experience some level of exhaustion. When we use fractionation, we go back and forth between topics of intensity and topics that are more casual. It's up to you which one you start with, but you should always make the transition natural. Go from casual jokes, to discussion about your families, to lighthearted banter about TV shows, to heartbreak, and so on.

Make sure the serious topics bring your feelings into play, and the lighthearted topics should be factual or humorous. This rollercoaster of moods will intensify the feeling of intimacy. The other person will feel like they've shared everything with you, and you will earn their trust.

- Make push and pull statements. When making statements that both push and pull a partner, it's important to keep both sides equal. Too much of a push, and they'll think you're a mean person or simply not interested. Too much of a pull, and they'll think you're needy and clingy. Push and pull statements allow you to express your feelings without overwhelming someone. When done right, they can pique interest and enhance desire.

To formulate the ideal statement for your situation, choose an aspect of their personality to compliment (don't make up a good quality - really choose one she embodies) and turn a conventional response on its head. For example, you could say, "I hate how amazing you are at guitar. It's such a blow to my ego." It's also important to deliver this line with humor and playfulness, so they perceive it as positive instead of negative. Another example of such a statement is, "You dress so well, I'm starting to think you shouldn't be seen with me." Whatever you choose to say, make sure it does not come across as an insult.

2. Insinuation

Quite simply, insinuation is the act of planting a thought or idea in someone's head. Instead of forcing a direction, you simply let this carefully-planted seed grow on its own. When we use insinuation to seduce, we allow the object of our desire a quick glimpse of what we have in mind.

- Touch a person briefly, especially when they aren't expecting it. We advise doing this on a part of the body that is bound to

send a tingle up their spine, though one should stay far away from all private regions. Lay a hand on the lower area of the back, affectionately rub someone's shoulder or grasp gently just above the knee.
- Make the occasional seductive glance, especially while keeping conversation light-hearted. Use your eyes to communicate how you truly feel, while your words stay in the safe zone.
- Use smart double entendres. The keyword here is 'smart.' Most people do not respond well to vulgar sexual innuendos, but a well-placed double entendre, at just the right time, can make a potential lover stir. It does not have to be sexual, it can be simply romantic. A double entendre is any statement that could have two meanings. If you're talking about your career, you could slip in the line, "I'm the kind of man who goes after what he wants and doesn't let go." This counts as a double entendre, since you could be talking about romantic pursuits as well. If you accompany this with an eye-gaze, you may just make the other person swoon. A sexual double entendre is a little riskier, but if you read the signals right, this could turn up the heat on your date.

3. Pauses

You know all about sexual tension, don't you? When we can't have someone exactly when we want them (and the feeling is mutual), our sense of desire grows and grows, until it's off-the-charts. As we've demonstrated, suspense enhances all emotion. And this is exactly why a well-timed and well-placed pause can be highly powerful. Here are some examples of when a pause can be effective.

- In a great compliment. Before you conclude the compliment, insert a pause that can be accompanied by eye-gazing or a shy smile. Let's say you're complimenting your current crush. You could say, "You look... stunning." This pause makes the compliment seem a lot more thoughtful and genuine, like you really thought about it, instead of just blurting it out.

- In a vulnerable statement. If you're discussing or explaining something in the realm of feelings, add a pause before the most revealing part of your sentence. This will add to the intimacy and vulnerability of the situation. If you're on a promising date, you could say, "I feel… like this is really going well." Pause. "Do you feel the same way?"

Six Highly Effective Tips for Successful Negotiations

Negotiations most commonly happen with our employers or managers, but they are not restricted to the professional realm. When we're young, we may negotiate with our parents, and once we're older, we may negotiate with our partners. The sign of a successful negotiation is both parties walking away satisfied. Someone's goal is reached and the other side does not feel lesser for it. The other party may even feel it's for the best. To ensure your future negotiations are providing you and the people in your life with maximum benefits, keep these tips in mind.

1. **Make timing your ally**

Pay close attention to the frame of mind your negotiation will be met with. Timing can make all the difference between a successful deal and one that misses the mark. If you try to negotiate with someone who is rushing to another appointment, just heard bad news, or just finished a heated argument with another person, you are very likely not going to get the response you want.

2. **Do not use submissive or weak language**

When you find yourself in this situation with a superior, it may be tempting to use submissive language to soften your request. Before you begin negotiating, you may want to say "I hate to ask you this but…" or "I hope this isn't too much but…" so you don't come across as demanding. This can actually weaken your request. If the opposing negotiator has a streak of arrogance, they may even use your disclaimer against you and act more aggressive. Do not give them fodder to do that with. Be confident and assertive, knowing your full value. Avoid acting submissive but also steer clear of acting entitled. Find a balance between the two.

3. **Share honest information**

When you're in this situation, especially in a professional setting, it can be easy to feel like you should be guarded. This isn't true. Being honest with your employer or other authority figure can actually help your case. For example, if you need a raise because you feel you're not getting what you're worth, and perhaps you've started to struggle financially, this can give your boss more incentive to give you what you want.

4. **Always have a first offer in mind**

You're in a vulnerable position, so it's only natural to cringe at making the first offer. You may also think that it's wise to feel out the situation before any numbers are cast. Studies have shown, however, that those who make the first offer get closer to their goal. If you're looking for a raise, you're more likely to get your target salary if you have an offer in mind. This is because the first offer is what the negotiations revolve around. Instead of bending yourself to your employer's offer, they will bend themselves to yours. The first offer anchors the situation, so make sure it's yours.

5. **Be brave with your offer**

Make sure that your offer is not too low. People are often afraid to ask for too much, but studies have actually shown that you're more likely to low-ball yourself. Reflect on what your ideal outcome is and do not feel obligated to play it safe. Your ideal outcome may be more possible than you think!

6. Consider what they would gain from saying 'yes'

You can't walk into a room and just make demands. Unless the other party has something to gain from meeting your demands, you can kiss their cooperation goodbye. Before negotiating, consider the extent of their gain to figure out just how much you'll be able to ask for. This gain could be anything, from receiving better performance or improved efforts from you. Or perhaps the benefit is keeping you instead of losing you.

Don't shy away from using conversation to get what you want. The reality is: everyone is doing it. And guess what? You probably are too – just subconsciously. When we act subconsciously, our actions are not under our control, and anything could happen. Take control now and start getting the outcomes you desire.

Conclusion

Congratulations on making it to the end of *Conversation Skills 2.0*! You should be proud of yourself and your newfound abilities. Social interactions can seem complex and overwhelming, but the new knowledge you've gleaned has placed you leagues ahead of the rest.

It's not that complicated once you break it down, is it? You'd do well to remember the big three rewards that we all look for in our human connections: safety, significance, and expansion. For the best outcomes, make your new acquaintances feel like they can trust you, like you appreciate them, and as though you have the ability to expand their horizons in some way, even if it's through humor and entertainment. Everything is grounded in these three major needs. Try and always satisfy them.

You've learned how to display likable behavior and give yourself an advantage for all proceeding conversations. In no time, you'll be brightening up a room and attracting connections like never before. You've also gained the tools for igniting interesting interactions, building magnetism, and developing deeper relationships with new and existing connections. And in addition to all of this, you've armored up for difficult social scenarios and learned persuasion techniques for a variety of social arenas.

Remember that it all begins with you. Learn to love yourself, stay true to who you are, and embrace your unique qualities. When we're comfortable with who we are, we let others in and we have more to offer them in our everyday conversations. Do what needs to be done to replenish your self-esteem and you'll easily stay a top-dog in your social interactions.

Another teaching I want you to take away is this: human beings are not as difficult as you think they are. Don't approach them with hesitation or fear. They are more similar to you than you realize, they've just accumulated different layers.

We can all be likened to locked treasure chests, filled with all manner of curious and fascinating things. Approach other humans the way you'd approach a locked treasure chest; take the time to find the right key and don't feel discouraged if one doesn't work. With patience, kindness, openness, and respect, try to experiment with different ways to open this box. What you find inside could be a great reward.

Human beings are social animals, so when we master conversation skills, connections are amplified and self-satisfaction becomes the new norm. Isn't that a reality you'd like to see?

www.ingramcontent.com/pod-product-compliance
Lightning Source LLC
Chambersburg PA
CBHW021128080526
44587CB00012B/1179